# decadent
# Desserts

Cover Photo: Almond Pumpkin Cheesecake, page 43

Pictured at right:

Top: Peach Bourbon Dessert, page 160
Bottom: Sticky Ginger Fig Cake, page 160

Decadent Desserts
Copyright © Company's Coming Publishing Limited

First Printing October 2003

**National Library of Canada Cataloguing in Publication**

Paré, Jean
    Decadent desserts / Jean Paré.

(Special occasion series)
Includes index.
ISBN 1-896891-60-8

    1. Desserts.  I. Title.  II. Series: Paré, Jean, 1927- . Special occasion series.

TX773.P35909 2003          641.8'6          C2003-902959-X

Published by
COMPANY'S COMING PUBLISHING LIMITED
2311 – 96 Street
Edmonton, Alberta, Canada T6N 1G3
Tel: (780) 450-6223          Fax: (780) 450-1857
companyscoming.com

Company's Coming is a registered trademark owned by Company's Coming Publishing Limited

Printing and binding by
Friesens, Altona, Manitoba, Canada

Printed in Canada

*Decadent Desserts* was created thanks
to the dedicated efforts of the people
and organizations listed below.

### COMPANY'S COMING PUBLISHING LIMITED

| | |
|---:|:---|
| Author | Jean Paré |
| President | Grant Lovig |
| Production Manager | Derrick Sorochan |
| Senior Designer | Zoë Henry |
| Publishing Coordinator | Shelly Willsey |

### THE RECIPE FACTORY

| | |
|---:|:---|
| Research & Development Manager | Nora Prokop |
| Editor | Laurel Hoffmann |
| Editorial Assistant | Rendi Dennis |
| Associate Editors | Stephanie Amodio |
| | Josie Wong |
| Copywriter | Debbie Dixon |
| Proofreaders | Audrey Carroll |
| | Audrey Dahl |
| | Connie Townsend |
| Food Editors | Lynda Elsenheimer |
| | Lovoni Walker |
| Test Kitchen Supervisor | Jessica Assaly |
| Test Kitchen Staff | James Bullock |
| | Sandra Clydesdale |
| Photo Editor | Patricia Meili-Bullock |
| Photographer | Stephe Tate Photo |
| Prep Kitchen Coordinator | Audrey Smetaniuk |
| Prep Kitchen Assistant | Linda Dobos |
| Prop Stylist | Snezana Ferenac |
| Registered Dietitian | Margaret Ng |

We gratefully acknowledge the following suppliers for their
generous support of our Test Kitchen and Photo Studio:

Broil King Barbecues
Corelle®
Hamilton Beach®
Lagostina®
Proctor Silex®
Tupperware®

Our special thanks to the following businesses for providing
extensive props for photography:

| | |
|---:|:---|
| Anchor Hocking Canada | Linens 'N Things |
| Baker's Secret® | Michaels The Arts And Crafts Store |
| Browne & Co. Ltd. | Mikasa Home Store |
| Canhome Global | Pfaltzgraff Canada |
| Casa Bugatti | Pyrex® Bakeware |
| Cherison Enterprises Inc. | Stokes |
| Danesco Inc. | The Bay |
| Dansk Gifts | Wiltshire® |
| Klass Works | Winners |
| La Cache | |

# Table of Contents

*Table of Contents*

# Foreword

*Decadent Desserts* has been a fun book to create because it's all about the sweetest of feasts, sinfully rich flavours and the many entertaining ways to indulge in some culinary magic.

We set out to show you how simple it can be to make delicious, elegant desserts. Throughout this book, you'll find lots of helpful "how-to" pictures to help you master the more complicated aspects of preparation in an easy-to-follow way. Shortcuts, tips and a little sage wisdom, not only from myself, but also from our team of experienced cooks (we made the mistakes for you!) will turn you into a gourmet dessert chef in no time!

Desserts bearing the name "decadent" must be exactly that, and such treats are a wonderful way to make a meal even more special. Delve into the tantalizing textures that vary from light and airy to rich and dense to smooth and creamy. Delight in the inviting aromas and eye-catching colours. These desserts are a joy to create and a pleasure to eat. Forget about the worries in your day-to-day life and treat yourself and your guests to a special indulgence. These are the moments to savour!

The first section in this book is appropriately named *Before You Begin*. These pages offer valuable information on the equipment you will need and some special techniques that can spell success in the kitchen. Read up on some dessert-making basics, such as using a piping bag (see page 15) and working with chocolate (see page 17). Novice and experienced cooks alike will learn something new.

A world of luscious desserts lies waiting in the sections that follow, each featuring a different type of dessert. Whether you are in the mood for something warm, flaky and soft or something cool, creamy and cheesy, you will find it in one of these sections. Each recipe is beautifully pictured to help you make the perfect choice and to give you some great presentation ideas. Have fun, experiment and be creative!

The book culminates with *Finishing Touches*, the section that offers you a chance to tap into your artistic side while introducing a definite "wow" factor to your dessert. These decorative additions will enhance your desserts without overwhelming them. Some take practice and a little bit of patience to master, but the end result is well worth the effort. These eye-catching garnishes, elegant sauces and unique, custom-made platters will more than impress your guests— they'll be dazzled!

It has been a real pleasure making *Decadent Desserts*. It was more than just fun—we had an absolutely delicious time perfecting each recipe. Every day our test kitchen was filled with the inviting aroma of something sweet and wonderful. This book is truly special because there's a little bit of magic to be found in every recipe—the kind of magic that lifts spirits, invites laughter and casts worries aside. We had a sweet time while it lasted. Now, I'm happy to say, it's your turn.

*Jean Paré*

Each recipe has been analyzed using the most up-to-date version of the Canadian Nutrient File from Health Canada, which is based on the United States Department of Agriculture (USDA) Nutrient Database. If more than one ingredient is listed (such as "hard margarine or butter"), then the first ingredient is used in the analysis. Where an ingredient reads "sprinkle," "optional," or "for garnish," it is not included as part of the nutrition information.

Margaret Ng, B.Sc. (Hon.), M.A.
Registered Dietitian

# Before You Begin

This is an excellent starting point and a great way
to avoid unexpected challenges during a critical point
in your preparations. Take a moment to look through
the equipment lists and method suggestions
before moving on to the recipes.

# Glossary

*The following are brief descriptions of some of the more uncommon tools and equipment used throughout this book. Before you get started, review these descriptions and the corresponding pictures on pages 10 and 11.*

**Cake Comb:**

A flat, triangular decorating utensil (usually plastic or metal), with a variety of serrated edges for decorating the tops and sides of iced cakes (see pages 172 and 173). A fork or serrated knife can also be used for this purpose.

**Jelly Roll Pan:**

A small 10 × 15 inch (25 × 38 cm) baking sheet with 1 inch (2.5 cm) sides. Can be used as a cookie sheet and for sheet cakes, sponge cakes or jelly rolls.

**Mandoline (pronounced MAN-duh-lihn):**

A small slicing machine with adjustable blades (also known as a slicer). Used to cut firm fruits or vegetables into thick or thin slices. Also great for julienne and french-fry cuts.

**Offset Spatula:**

A narrow, flat, metal utensil that is bent upward near the handle. Excellent for spreading icing on cakes (see page 172) and for lifting delicate items.

**Parchment Paper (also known as silicone paper):**

A moisture-resistant, non-stick paper used for lining baking pans and making disposable piping bags. Also reusable—clean by wiping with a damp cloth. Discard when it becomes dark or heavily soiled. Available in large rolls/sheets that can be cut to fit any pan size.

**Pastry Brush:**

A small brush used for applying melted butter or egg washes onto pastries and other baked goods. Look for a good-quality nylon or natural bristle brush.

**Ramekin (pronounced RAM-ih-kihn):**

A small, round baking dish used for individual portions, usually made of porcelain or earthenware. Looks like a miniature soufflé dish. These inexpensive dishes can be used for desserts such as custards, mousses or puddings. Available with straight or slightly sloped sides.

**Springform Pan:**

A round metal pan with a high, straight, expandable side equipped with spring-loaded hinge. The bottom is easily removed from the side by releasing the hinge, making it easy to remove cakes, tortes and cheesecakes from the pan. Available in at least 3 different sizes (8 inch, 20 cm; 9 inch, 22 cm; and 10 inch, 25 cm).

**Tart Pan:**

A metal baking pan with a removable bottom and low sides which are fluted.

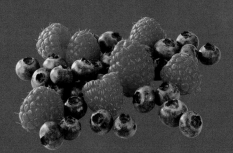

# Baking Equipment

1. Bundt pan
2. Muffin pan
3. Deep cake pan
4. Springform pan
5. Jelly mold
6. Pie plate
7. Round cake pan
8. Square cake pan
9. Deep tart pan with removable bottom
10. Custard cups
11. Straight-sided ramekins
12. Baking sheet with sides
13. Jelly roll pan
14. Tart pan with removable bottom
15. Rectangular tart pan with removable bottom

# Baking Tools

1. Mandoline/Slicer
2. Strainer
3. Chopper
4. Box grater
5. Piping bag
6. Closed star piping tip
7. Open star piping tip
8. Plain piping tip
9. Fine strainer
10. Chef's knife

11. Serrated knife
12. Paring knife
13. Vegetable peeler
14. Juicer
15. Metal tongs
16. Oven thermometer
17. Meat mallet
18. Small offset spatula
19. Small spatula
20. Large offset spatula

21. Large spatula
22. Rubber spatulas
23. Rolling pin
24. Kitchen timer
25. Whisk – silicone covered
26. Whisk
27. Egg separator
28. Pizza cutter
29. Pastry brushes
30. Pastry cutter

# Lining Pans

*Learn how to line even the trickiest pan to prevent your baking efforts from sticking.*

**Round:** Cut strip of parchment (not waxed) paper height of pan and 1 inch (2.5 cm) longer than circumference of pan. Grease bottom and side of pan. Press paper onto inside edge of pan. Trace circle on parchment (not waxed) paper using pan as guide. Cut out. Lay in bottom of pan.

**Springform:** Turn removable bottom of pan upside down (invert bottom). Grease bottom and side of pan. Trace circle on parchment (not waxed) paper using pan as guide. Cut out. Lay in bottom of pan. Secure side.

Cut strip of parchment (not waxed) paper height of pan and 1 inch (2.5 cm) longer than circumference of pan. Press paper onto inside edge of pan.

**Square:** Cut 2 pieces of parchment (not waxed) paper height and length of sides of pan. Cut another piece of parchment (not waxed) paper length of 2 sides and bottom of pan, making paper extend over 2 sides. Grease bottom and sides of pan. Press paper onto bottom and sides of pan.

**Jelly roll:** Grease bottom and sides of pan. Line bottom and sides of jelly roll pan with parchment (not waxed paper), making paper extend 2 inches (5 cm) over long sides.

# Cutting Even Layers

*Cutting a cake into even layers is easier than it sounds. Here are a few tricks of the trade that will help you to achieve professional results every time.*

**Trimming:** Use serrated knife to cut domed top from cake, creating a flat even surface.

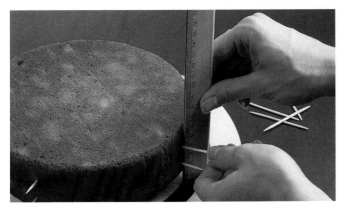

**Marking:** Use 2 wooden picks to mark cake into 3 equal layers in 4 to 6 places around outside edge of cake.

**Note:** Use a Lazy Susan to make it easier to cut cake evenly.

**Cutting With Knife:** Holding serrated knife against cake, using wooden picks as guide, slowly turn Lazy Susan around to make 2 lines of equal distance around cake. Cut through cake using lines as guide.

**Cutting With String or Thread:** Cut piece of fine string or strong thread about 5 inches (12.5 cm) longer than circumference of cake. Place string around outside edge of cake on wooden picks. Bring both ends of string around to front of cake. Cross ends of strings in front and firmly, but carefully, pull them in opposite directions, going back through cake. Repeat to create additional layer.

# Forming Tart Crusts

*Fit your pastry into a tart pan
with ease using this clever technique.*

**Lining Tart Pan:** Roll out pastry on lightly floured surface until large enough to fit into tart pan. Place rolling pin on pastry end closest to you. Roll part of pastry up and over rolling pin. Gently roll pastry around rolling pin to lift from surface. Carefully unroll pastry over tart pan, using rolling pin as a guide.

Using small ball of leftover pastry, press pastry into pan to create fluted edge.

Trim edge of pastry by pressing rolling pin across top edge of tart pan. Remove scraps.

# Blind Baking

*This is a great way to pre-bake your crusts
and prevent them from rising unevenly.*

Place sheet of parchment paper (or foil) over crust, bringing paper up over side of pan. Fill halfway up side with dried beans or rice. Bake in 375°F (190°C) oven for 15 minutes.

Carefully remove paper and beans or rice. (These can be kept for next time you are baking pastry.) Finish baking crust for about 10 minutes until lightly browned. Cool.

# Piping Basics

*Your piping bag will quickly become your best friend as you delve into the world of dessert decorating. Once you have mastered these simple skills, there is no end to the fun you can have with this tool. See page 176 to make a paper piping cone.*

Place coupler and desired tip in narrow end of empty piping bag. Place bag, tip end down, in glass that comes about halfway up side of bag. Fold excess fabric over glass. Spoon mixture into bag.

Twist top of bag. Secure twist between thumb and forefinger. Squeeze top of bag with firm, even pressure. Guide tip with other hand.

**Piping Rosettes:** Fill empty piping bag fitted with small open star tip. Fill as directed on this page. Squeeze bag gently as you pipe in a circular motion to create rosette.

**Piping Circles:** Place large plain tip in empty piping bag. Fill as directed on this page. Hold bag at slight angle or straight up so tip is directly over desired piping area. Gently squeeze bag while "drawing" a circle with meringue, working from the outside in.

# Sugar Basics

*Sugar mixtures must always be heated with a watchful eye, as sugar can burn very easily. Make sure you aren't distracted during this step.*

**Sugar Syrup:** Combine 2 cups (500 mL) sugar and 1 cup (250 mL) water in medium saucepan. Heat and stir on medium-low until sugar is dissolved. Brush side of pan to remove any sugar mixture that may have splashed up. This helps to prevent the sugar from crystalizing.

Boil, uncovered, on medium-high for 5 to 10 minutes, without stirring, until deep golden brown colour. Be sure to watch carefully and immediately remove pan from heat once colour is reached.

# Making Praline

*Pronounced PRAY-leen (or PRAH-leen), this sweet, brittle mixture is made from nuts and caramelized sugar. Originating in France in 1671, praline was discovered quite by accident. As dessert was being prepared for the Duke of Plesslis-Praslin, a bowl of almonds spilled onto the floor. In the chaos, the chef also spilled a pot of burnt sugar onto the almonds. The Duke was anxious for his dessert so, out of desperation, his personal chef served him the sugar-coated almonds. They were a hit! The Duke liked the sweet dessert so much, he named it Praslin, after himself. Today, praline is broken into pieces and enjoyed as candy or ground up and used in desserts as an ingredient or garnish.*

Spread nuts in single layer, touching, on lightly greased baking sheet. Pour sugar mixture evenly over nuts. Let stand for about 20 minutes until hard.

Break into pieces. Process in food processor until coarse crumbs or put into plastic bag and crush with mallet or rolling pin.

# Peeling Hazelnuts

*The time-consuming task of peeling hazelnuts is made easy with this valuable method.*

Spread hazelnuts evenly in ungreased shallow pan. Bake in 350°F (175°C) oven for 5 to 10 minutes, stirring or shaking often, until fragrant.

Spread toasted hazelnuts on one half of tea towel. Fold other half over to cover nuts. Rub vigorously back and forth for 1 to 2 minutes, pressing down until almost all skins are removed. You may not be able to remove all skins of hazelnuts, but outer paper skins should come off.

# Melting Chocolate

*You will work with chocolate with confidence once you have reviewed these simple concepts.*

**Stovetop Melting Method:** Break or chop chocolate into small, reasonably uniform-sized pieces. Heat in heavy saucepan on lowest heat, stirring often, until almost melted. Do not overheat. Remove from heat. Stir until smooth.

**Microwave Melting Method:** Break or chop chocolate into small, reasonably uniform-sized pieces. Put into microwave-safe bowl. Microwave, uncovered, on medium (50%) for 30 second intervals until chocolate is almost melted. Stir until smooth.

### Additional Tips:

- Don't rush melting process. Chocolate requires very low heat to melt properly. Too high heat will cause chocolate to seize.

- Remove chocolate from heat before melted completely. Residual heat will continue to melt it completely while stirring.

- Never cover saucepan on stove or bowl in microwave when melting chocolate. Condensation forming on inside of lid or cover will cause chocolate to seize.

- When melting chocolate, keep water away. One drop of water can cause chocolate to seize.

# Cakes & Tortes

These stunning recipes will rise to any occasion!
Their sheer decadence makes them perfect for a special
celebration. Choose from a wonderful selection of cakes,
or broaden your culinary experience by making
a unique and delicious torte.

# Extreme Chocolate Cake

*A chocolate lover's dream! The cake is moist with a decadent, melt-in-your-mouth texture.*

| | | |
|---|---|---|
| Cocoa, for dusting | | |
| Dark chocolate cake mix (2 layer size) | 1 | 1 |
| Instant chocolate pudding powder (4 serving size) | 1 | 1 |
| Large eggs | 4 | 4 |
| Cooking oil | 1/2 cup | 125 mL |
| Warm water | 1/2 cup | 125 mL |
| Sour cream | 1 cup | 250 mL |
| Semi-sweet chocolate chips | 1 1/2 cups | 375 mL |
| **CHOCOLATE GANACHE (GLAZE)** | | |
| Whipping cream | 1/2 cup | 125 mL |
| Bittersweet chocolate baking squares (1 oz., 28 g, each), coarsely chopped | 5 | 5 |

Grease 12 cup (2.7 L) bundt pan. Dust with cocoa. Beat next 6 ingredients in large bowl on low for 2 minutes, scraping down side 2 or 3 times. Beat on medium for about 2 minutes until smooth.

Stir in chocolate chips. Turn into prepared pan. Spread evenly. Bake in 350°F (175°C) oven for 60 to 70 minutes until wooden pick inserted in centre comes out without batter on it, but will have chocolate from the chocolate chips. Let stand in pan on wire rack for 20 minutes before inverting onto serving plate to cool completely.

**Chocolate Ganache (Glaze):** Heat whipping cream in heavy small saucepan on medium until boiling. Remove from heat.

Add chocolate. Stir slowly for about 2 minutes until melted completely. Cool for 5 to 10 minutes, stirring occasionally, until slightly thickened, but still pourable. If chocolate gets too stiff, set saucepan in hot water for 1 to 2 minutes until desired consistency. Makes 1 cup (250 mL) ganache. Slowly pour over top of cake, allowing some to run partially down sides. Let set before cutting. Cuts into 16 wedges.

*1 wedge: 412 Calories; 25.8 g Total Fat (10.7 g Mono, 4.3 g Poly, 9.4 g Sat); 69 mg Cholesterol; 47 g Carbohydrate; 2 g Fibre; 5 g Protein; 392 mg Sodium*

Pictured below.

# Lemon Cheese Coconut Cake

*This attractive cake has a very pretty feathered design in the icing. Create a different look by using any colour, or colours, you choose.*

| All-purpose flour | 1 2/3 cups | 400 mL |
|---|---|---|
| Granulated sugar | 1 cup | 250 mL |
| Medium coconut | 1/2 cup | 125 mL |
| Ground almonds | 1/3 cup | 75 mL |
| Baking powder | 1 tbsp. | 15 mL |
| Buttermilk (or reconstituted from powder) | 1 cup | 250 mL |
| Butter (or hard margarine), melted | 1/2 cup | 125 mL |
| Large eggs | 2 | 2 |
| Vanilla | 1 tsp. | 5 mL |

### LEMON CREAM CHEESE FILLING

| Block of cream cheese, softened | 8 oz. | 250 g |
|---|---|---|
| Icing (confectioner's) sugar | 3/4 cup | 175 mL |
| Finely grated lemon zest | 2 tsp. | 10 mL |
| Lemon juice | 1 tbsp. | 15 mL |
| Medium coconut, toasted (see Tip, below) | 3/4 cup | 175 mL |

### GLACÉ (ICING)

| Icing (confectioner's) sugar | 1 1/4 cups | 300 mL |
|---|---|---|
| Butter (or hard margarine), softened | 1 tbsp. | 15 mL |
| Milk | 2 tbsp. | 30 mL |
| Drop of yellow food colouring | 1 | 1 |
| Drop of red food colouring | 1 | 1 |

Grease 8 inch (20 cm) springform pan. Combine first 5 ingredients in large bowl. Make a well in centre.

Put next 4 ingredients into 2 cup (500 mL) liquid measure. Mix. Pour into well. Stir until smooth. Pour batter into prepared pan. Spread evenly. Bake in 350°F (175°C) oven for about 1 hour until wooden pick inserted in centre comes out clean. Let stand in pan for 10 minutes before removing to wire rack to cool completely. Cut cake horizontally into 2 equal layers (see page 13).

**Lemon Cream Cheese Filling:** Beat first 4 ingredients in large bowl until smooth. Makes 1 1/3 cups (325 mL) filling. Put 1 cake layer onto small round cake board (see page 184). Spread 1/3 of filling on top of cake. Place second layer on top. Spread remaining filling around side of cake, leaving top uniced.

Lightly press coconut into filling around side of cake (see page 173).

**Glacé (Icing):** Combine icing sugar, butter and enough milk to make thick, barely pourable mixture. Makes 2/3 cup (150 mL) glacé. Put 1 tbsp. (15 mL) glacé into each of 2 small bowls. Spread remaining glacé evenly over top of cake.

Add 1 drop of food colouring to glacé in each bowl. Stir well. Put yellow glacé into small piping bag fitted with small plain nozzle. Pipe straight lines, about 1 1/2 inches (3.8 cm) apart, across top of cake. Put pink glacé into cleaned piping bag. Pipe straight lines in between yellow lines.

Drag wooden pick or skewer through lines in 1 direction. Repeat in opposite direction, 1 inch (2.5 cm) from first line. Continue across cake, changing directions for each line. Cuts into 10 wedges.

1 wedge: 566 Calories; 30 g Total Fat (7.2 g Mono, 1.3 g Poly, 19.7 g Sat); 101 mg Cholesterol; 69 g Carbohydrate; 1 g Fibre; 8 g Protein; 343 mg Sodium

Pictured on page 21.

---

To toast nuts and seeds, spread evenly in ungreased shallow pan. Bake in 350°F (175°C) oven for 5 to 10 minutes, stirring or shaking often, until desired doneness.

# Mocha Mud Cake

*This inviting chocolate cake coated with a rich mocha icing.
Find three reasons to try each of the eye-catching
decorating options. This elegant cake can
be made and decorated a day ahead
and chilled until ready to serve.*

| | | |
|---|---|---|
| Butter (or hard margarine), cut up | 1 cup | 250 mL |
| Water | 1 cup | 250 mL |
| Granulated sugar | 1 cup | 250 mL |
| Semi-sweet chocolate baking squares (1 oz., 28 g, each), chopped | 8 | 8 |
| Instant coffee granules | 1 tbsp. | 15 mL |
| All-purpose flour | 1 cup | 250 mL |
| Baking powder | 1 1/2 tsp. | 7 mL |
| Cocoa, sifted if lumpy | 1/4 cup | 60 mL |
| Large eggs, fork-beaten | 2 | 2 |
| **COFFEE BUTTERCREAM ICING** | | |
| Butter (or hard margarine), softened | 1 1/3 cups | 325 mL |
| Icing (confectioner's) sugar | 2/3 cup | 150 mL |
| Instant coffee granules | 2 tbsp. | 30 mL |
| Warm water | 3 tbsp. | 50 mL |
| **DECORATION 1 (optional)** | | |
| Sliced almonds (with skins), toasted (see Tip, page 20) | 1 cup | 250 mL |
| **DECORATION 2 (optional)** | | |
| Cocoa, for dusting | 1/4 – 1/2 cup | 60 – 125 mL |
| Chocolate orange sticks (about 1 1/4 boxes, 4 oz., 125 g, each) | 50 | 50 |
| **DECORATION 3 (optional)** | | |
| White chocolate baking squares (1 oz., 28 g, each) | 4 | 4 |
| Cooking oil | 1 tsp. | 5 mL |
| Block of dark chocolate | 1/2 lb. | 225 g |

Grease 9 inch (22 cm) springform pan (see Note). Line bottom and side with parchment (not waxed) paper (see page 12). Combine first 5 ingredients in heavy large saucepan. Heat on lowest heat, stirring often, until chocolate is almost melted. Do not overheat. Remove from heat. Stir until smooth.

Add next 3 ingredients. Whisk until smooth.

Add eggs. Stir well. Pour into prepared pan. Spread evenly. Bake in 325°F (160°C) oven for 40 minutes. Cover loosely with foil. Bake for 20 to 35 minutes until set. A wooden pick inserted in centre should come out sticky, but not wet. Let stand in pan on wire rack until cooled completely. Remove from pan to serving plate. (Set on small cake board first if doing Decoration 1. See page 184.)

**Coffee Buttercream Icing:** Beat butter until light and creamy. Gradually add icing sugar. Beat until smooth and fluffy.

Combine coffee granules and warm water in small cup. Add to butter mixture. Beat well. Makes 2 cups (500 mL) icing. Spread top and side of cake with icing. Choose one of the following decoration ideas below. Cuts into 12 wedges.

1 wedge: 579 Calories; 44.6 g Total Fat (13.2 g Mono, 1.8 g Poly, 27.3 g Sat); 138 mg Cholesterol; 46 g Carbohydrate; 2 g Fibre; 4 g Protein; 445 mg Sodium

**Note:** To prevent cake batter from leaking out of springform pan, use a pan with a secure/tight-fitting base. Or set pan on sheet of foil and firmly press foil up around side of pan.

**Decoration 1:** Use serrated knife, cake comb or fork to make wavy lines in icing on top of cake.

Press almonds around side of cake to cover completely. Chill.

Pictured on page 24.

**Decoration 2:** Place paper doily on top of cake. Dust top with cocoa, filling in all exposed areas. Gently lift off doily.

**Decoration 3:** Cut piece of parchment (not waxed) paper same height as cake and long enough to go around circumference of cake plus 1/2 inch (12 mm) for "tab." A decorative edge may be added. Secure to counter with tape. Heat white chocolate in heavy small saucepan on lowest heat, stirring often, until almost melted. Do not overheat. Remove from heat. Stir until smooth. Add cooking oil. Stir. Spread mixture smoothly on paper with offset spatula, leaving "tab" uncovered. Let stand for 1 to 4 minutes until slightly set, but still pliable. If chocolate becomes too set for shaping, use low setting on hair dryer to warm chocolate until pliable enough.

Cut orange sticks in half. Place vertically around side of cake. Make curls with orange stick. Place onto centre of cake.

Pictured on page 24/25.

Working quickly, wrap collar around cake, gently pressing ends to meet together. Do not remove paper. Let stand for 1 hour. Carefully peel off and discard paper.

To cut dense chocolate cake or cake with chocolate collar, run sharp knife with long blade under hot water. Blot quickly. The hot metal blade will melt chocolate as it is cut to make perfect, even slices. Use hot, clean knife for each cut.

Peel wide curls from chocolate block directly onto top of cake to form pile in middle (see page 177).

Pictured on page 25.

**Photo legend next page:**
Mocha Mud Cake, page 22
  Top Left: Decoration 1
  Centre: Decoration 2
  Top Right: Decoration 3

# Orange Layered Cake

*This moist cake has a tempting citrus flavour enclosed in a creamy icing. Decorative White Chocolate Tiles add an extra touch of elegance.*

| | | |
|---|---|---|
| Butter (or hard margarine), softened | 1 cup | 250 mL |
| Granulated sugar | 1 cup | 250 mL |
| Large eggs | 4 | 4 |
| Finely grated orange zest | 2 tbsp. | 30 mL |
| Vanilla | 2 tsp. | 10 mL |
| All-purpose flour | 2 1/2 cups | 625 mL |
| Baking powder | 4 tsp. | 20 mL |
| Milk | 3/4 cup | 175 mL |

**WHITE CHOCOLATE TILES (optional)**

| | | |
|---|---|---|
| White chocolate baking squares (1 oz., 28 g, each), chopped | 12 | 12 |
| Cooking oil | 1/2 tsp. | 2 mL |

**ORANGE WHITE CHOCOLATE ICING**

| | | |
|---|---|---|
| Orange juice | 3/4 cup | 175 mL |
| White chocolate bars (3 1/2 oz., 100 g, each), chopped | 3 | 3 |
| Butter (not margarine), softened | 1 1/2 cups | 375 mL |
| Icing (confectioner's) sugar | 1 cup | 250 mL |
| Finely grated orange zest | 1 tbsp. | 15 mL |

Grease deep 8 inch (20 cm) round cake pan (see Note). Line bottom and side with parchment (not waxed) paper (see page 12). Beat butter and sugar in large bowl until light and fluffy. Add eggs, 1 at a time, beating well after each addition. Add orange zest and vanilla. Beat well.

Combine flour and baking powder in medium bowl. Add flour mixture to egg mixture alternately with milk. Stir until smooth. Spoon batter into prepared pan. Spread evenly. Bake in 350°F (175°C) oven for about 1 hour until wooden pick inserted in centre comes out clean. Let stand in pan for 10 minutes before inverting onto wire rack to cool completely. Cut cake horizontally into 3 equal layers (see page 13).

**White Chocolate Tiles:** Heat chocolate in heavy medium saucepan on lowest heat, stirring often, until almost melted (see page 17). Do not overheat. Remove from heat.

Add cooking oil. Stir until smooth.

Cut 4 pieces of parchment (not waxed) paper, each 3 1/4 x 12 inches (8 x 30 cm). Secure to counter with tape. Divide and spread chocolate evenly with offset spatula. Let stand until set. Cut crosswise into 1 1/2 inch (3.8 cm) pieces. Makes 32 tiles.

**Orange White Chocolate Icing:** Heat orange juice and chocolate in heavy small saucepan on lowest heat, stirring often, until chocolate is almost melted. Do not overheat. Remove from heat. Stir until smooth. Cool completely.

Beat butter in large bowl until light and creamy. Add icing sugar, 1 tbsp. (15 mL) at a time, beating until sugar is dissolved and mixture is thick and white. Beat in chocolate mixture until thick and fluffy.

Stir in orange zest. Mix well. Makes 4 cups (1 L) icing. Place 1 cake layer on serving plate. Spread with 1 cup (250 mL) icing. Place second cake layer on top. Spread with 1 cup (250 mL) icing. Add remaining cake layer. Cover top and side of cake with remaining icing. Spread top evenly with spatula to form small peaks (see page 172).

Remove tiles from paper, 1 at a time, and press around side of cake, with each tile overlapping about 1/3 inch (1 cm).

1 wedge: 744 Calories; 50.3 g Total Fat (14.8 g Mono, 2.1 g Poly, 30.3 g Sat); 187 mg Cholesterol; 68 g Carbohydrate; 1 g Fibre; 8 g Protein; 589 mg Sodium

Pictured on page 27.

**Note:** Deep cake pans are available in kitchen and craft stores and some department stores. An 8 inch (20 cm) springform pan may be used. To prevent batter from leaking out of springform pan, use pan with a secure/tight-fitting base. Or set pan on sheet of foil and firmly press foil up around side of pan.

# Carrot Cream Cheese Roll

*This lighter-textured spice cake is very satisfying. A decadent version of the more traditional cake. Freezes well.*

| Large eggs | 4 | 4 |
| --- | --- | --- |
| Granulated sugar | 1 cup | 250 mL |
| Salt | 1/4 tsp. | 1 mL |
| Vanilla | 1 tsp. | 5 mL |
| All-purpose flour | 1 cup | 250 mL |
| Baking powder | 2 tsp. | 10 mL |
| Cocoa, sifted if lumpy | 2 tsp. | 10 mL |
| Ground cinnamon | 1 tsp. | 5 mL |
| Grated carrot | 1 cup | 250 mL |
| Water | 1/4 cup | 60 mL |
| Icing (confectioner's) sugar | 1/2 cup | 125 mL |

**CREAM CHEESE FILLING**

| Block of cream cheese, softened | 8 oz. | 250 g |
| --- | --- | --- |
| Butter (or hard margarine), softened | 1/2 cup | 125 mL |
| Vanilla (white vanilla is best) | 2 tsp. | 10 mL |
| Icing (confectioner's) sugar | 4 cups | 1 L |
| Raisins, coarsely chopped | 1/2 cup | 125 mL |
| Finely chopped walnuts | 1/4 cup | 60 mL |
| Finely chopped walnuts, for garnish | 1/4 cup | 60 mL |

Grease 10 x 15 inch (25 x 38 cm) jelly roll pan. Line with parchment (not waxed) paper, extending paper 2 inches (5 cm) over long sides (see page 12). Beat eggs in small bowl until frothy. Add granulated sugar, 1 tbsp. (15 mL) at a time, beating well after each addition until thick and sugar is dissolved. This will take about 10 minutes. Add salt and vanilla. Beat well. Transfer to large bowl.

Sift flour, baking powder, cocoa and cinnamon over egg mixture, 1/2 at a time, folding gently in between until no dry flour remains.

Fold in carrot and water. Turn into prepared pan. Spread evenly. Bake in 350°F (175°C) oven for 15 to 20 minutes until wooden pick inserted in centre comes out clean. Let stand in pan on wire rack for 5 minutes. Run knife along sides to loosen.

Spread large tea towel on counter. Cover with sheet of parchment (or waxed) paper. Sift icing sugar evenly over paper. Invert cake onto icing sugar. Carefully peel off and discard original parchment paper. Roll up from short end using towel and paper as guide. Let stand for about 10 minutes until cooled completely.

**Cream Cheese Filling:** Beat cream cheese, butter and vanilla in large bowl until fluffy. Gradually beat in icing sugar until smooth. Makes 3 cups (750 mL) filling. Unroll cake. Spread 1/2 of filling over cake to within 1 inch (2.5 cm) of each edge.

Sprinkle raisins and first amount of walnuts over filling. Roll up cake from short end, using towel and paper as guide. Trim ends. Place roll, seam-side down, on long 12 inch (30 cm) serving plate or cake board (see page 184). Spread with remaining filling.

Sprinkle with second amount of walnuts. Chill until ready to serve. Just before serving, cut with serrated knife, dampened with hot water, into 3/4 inch (2 cm) slices. Cuts into 12 slices.

1 slice: 507 Calories; 18.9 g Total Fat (5.4 g Mono, 1.9 g Poly, 10.3 g Sat); 117 mg Cholesterol; 81 g Carbohydrate; 1 g Fibre; 6 g Protein; 282 mg Sodium

Pictured on page 29.

# Chocolate Orange Mousse Cake

*What a treat! Dark chocolate cake layers, alternating with a rich mousse filling. Omit the chocolate collar around the cake if you prefer—it will still be delicious!*

| | | |
|---|---|---|
| Chocolate cake mix (2 layer size) | 1 | 1 |

**CHOCOLATE ORANGE MOUSSE**

| | | |
|---|---|---|
| Semi-sweet chocolate baking squares (1 oz., 28 g, each), chopped | 8 | 8 |
| Butter (or hard margarine) | 3 tbsp. | 50 mL |
| Egg yolks (large) | 3 | 3 |
| Finely grated orange zest | 1 tbsp. | 15 mL |
| Egg whites (large), room temperature | 3 | 3 |
| Whipping cream | 1 cup | 250 mL |
| Orange juice | 1/3 cup | 75 mL |
| Orange-flavoured liqueur (such as Grand Marnier) | 2 tbsp. | 30 mL |

**CHOCOLATE POLKA DOT COLLAR (optional)**

| | | |
|---|---|---|
| White chocolate baking square, chopped | 1 oz. | 28 g |
| Semi-sweet chocolate baking square, chopped | 1 oz. | 28 g |
| Milk chocolate bar, chopped | 3 1/2 oz. | 100 g |

Grease two 9 inch (22 cm) round cake pans. Prepare cake mix according to package directions. Pour into prepared pans. Spread evenly. Bake in 350°F (175°C) oven for 25 to 30 minutes until wooden pick inserted in centre comes out clean. Let stand for 10 minutes before inverting and removing onto wire racks to cool. Cut each cake horizontally into 2 equal layers (see page 13).

**Chocolate Orange Mousse:** Heat chocolate and butter in heavy small saucepan on lowest heat, stirring often, until chocolate is almost melted. Do not overheat. Remove from heat. Stir until smooth.

Add egg yolks and orange zest. Stir well. Turn into large bowl. Cover. Chill for 1 hour.

Beat egg whites in medium bowl until soft peaks form. Fold into chocolate mixture.

Beat whipping cream in small bowl until soft peaks form. Fold into chocolate mixture. Makes about 4 cups (1 L) mousse.

Combine orange juice and liqueur in separate small bowl. Place 1 cake layer on serving plate. Brush with orange juice mixture. Spread 1/4 of mousse evenly on top. Place second cake layer on top. Repeat layers, finishing with mousse layer. Cover. Chill for at least 6 hours or overnight.

**Chocolate Polka Dot Collar** (see how-to photos, page 174): Cut piece of parchment (not waxed) paper same height as cake and long enough to go around circumference of cake plus 1/2 inch (12 mm) for "tab." Secure to counter with tape. Heat white chocolate in heavy small saucepan on lowest heat, stirring often, until almost melted (see page 17). Do not overheat. Remove from heat. Stir until smooth. Cool slightly. Spoon into small piping bag fitted with small plain tip. Pipe dots, in various sizes, randomly onto parchment paper. Repeat with semi-sweet chocolate. Let stand for about 2 minutes until both chocolates are set.

Heat milk chocolate in heavy small saucepan on lowest heat, stirring often, until almost melted. Do not overheat. Remove from heat. Stir until smooth. Cool slightly. Carefully spread on parchment paper over chocolate dots with offset spatula, leaving "tab" uncovered. Let stand for 1 to 4 minutes until slightly set, but still pliable. If chocolate becomes too set for shaping, use low setting on hair dryer to warm chocolate until pliable enough. Working quickly, wrap collar around cake, gently pressing ends to meet together. Do not remove paper. Let stand for 1 hour. Carefully peel off and discard parchment paper. Cuts into 12 wedges.

1 wedge: 389 Calories; 23.2 g Total Fat (7.9 g Mono, 2.8 g Poly, 11.2 g Sat); 86 mg Cholesterol; 44 g Carbohydrate; 1 g Fibre; 5 g Protein; 406 mg Sodium

Pictured on page 31.

# Caramel Almond Torte

*The rum-flavoured syrup pools in the cracks that form on the top of this meringue and sponge layer cake. So luscious!*

### MERINGUE LAYERS

| | | |
|---|---|---|
| Egg whites (large), room temperature | 4 | 4 |
| Cream of tartar | 1/2 tsp. | 2 mL |
| Granulated sugar | 1 cup | 250 mL |
| Buttery cracker crumbs (such as Ritz) | 1 1/3 cups | 325 mL |
| Finely chopped almonds | 1 cup | 250 mL |

### CARAMEL ICING

| | | |
|---|---|---|
| Butter (or hard margarine) | 3/4 cup | 175 mL |
| Brown sugar, packed | 1 1/2 cups | 375 mL |
| Milk | 6 tbsp. | 100 mL |
| Icing (confectioner's) sugar | 3 cups | 750 mL |
| Milk | 6 tbsp. | 100 mL |
| Vanilla | 3/4 tsp. | 4 mL |

### SPONGE LAYERS

| | | |
|---|---|---|
| Butter (or hard margarine), softened | 6 tbsp. | 100 mL |
| Granulated sugar | 3/4 cup | 175 mL |
| Egg yolks (large) | 4 | 4 |
| Vanilla | 1/2 tsp. | 2 mL |
| Milk | 1/2 cup | 125 mL |
| All-purpose flour | 1 cup | 250 mL |
| Baking powder | 1 tsp. | 5 mL |
| Salt | 1/4 tsp. | 1 mL |

### SYRUP

| | | |
|---|---|---|
| Brown sugar, packed | 1 cup | 250 mL |
| Water | 1/3 cup | 75 mL |
| Rum flavouring | 1/2 tsp. | 2 mL |
| Sliced almonds (with skins), for garnish | 1/2 cup | 125 mL |

**Meringue Layers:** Grease bottoms of two 9 inch (22 cm) round cake pans. Line bottoms with parchment (not waxed) paper (see page 12). Beat egg whites and cream of tartar in large bowl until soft peaks form. Add sugar, 1 tbsp. (15 mL) at a time, beating well after each addition, until sugar is dissolved.

Fold in cracker crumbs and almonds. Divide and turn into prepared pans. Spread evenly. Bake in 325°F (160°C) oven for 25 to 30 minutes until dry. Let stand in pans for 30 minutes before removing to wire racks to cool completely.

**Caramel Icing:** Heat butter, brown sugar and first amount of milk in medium saucepan over medium, stirring constantly, until boiling. Boil for 3 minutes, without stirring. Cool to room temperature.

Add icing sugar, second amount of milk and vanilla. Stir, adding more milk as needed for easy spreading consistency. Makes about 3 1/3 cups (825 mL) icing. Set aside.

**Sponge Layers:** Grease two 9 inch (22 cm) round cake pans. Beat butter and sugar in medium bowl until creamy and light coloured. Add egg yolks, vanilla and milk. Beat well.

Combine flour, baking powder and salt in separate medium bowl. Add to butter mixture. Beat well. Stir until moistened. Turn into prepared pans. Spread evenly. Bake in 350°F (175°C) oven for about 25 minutes until wooden pick inserted in centre comes out clean. Let stand in pans for 5 minutes before removing to wire racks to cool completely.

**Syrup:** Heat brown sugar and water in medium saucepan on medium, stirring constantly, until boiling. Boil for 5 minutes, without stirring.

Stir in rum flavouring. Makes 2/3 cup (150 mL) syrup.

Assemble on serving plate as follows:

1. first meringue layer, bottom-side up
2. spread with 2/3 cup (150 mL) icing
3. first sponge layer
4. brush with syrup
5. spread with 2/3 cup (150 mL) icing
6. second sponge layer
7. brush with syrup
8. spread with 2/3 cup (150 mL) icing
9. second meringue layer, top-side up

Ice side of torte with remaining icing. Drizzle remaining syrup back and forth over top of torte, allowing some to run down side. Let stand, uncovered, at room temperature or chill for 6 hours until set and meringue top has softened slightly. Cover with plastic wrap. Chill for up to 4 days. Just before serving, garnish with almonds. Cuts into 12 wedges.

1 wedge: 777 Calories; 28.5 g Total Fat (10.8 g Mono, 3 g Poly, 13 g Sat); 122 mg Cholesterol; 128 g Carbohydrate; 1 g Fibre; 7 g Protein; 399 mg Sodium

Pictured on page 33.

# Lemon Poppy Seed Torte

*Fluffy lemon icing surrounds the soft poppy seed layers.*
*Each bite is both tart and sweet.*

## POPPY SEED SHEET CAKE

| | | |
|---|---|---|
| Homogenized milk | 1 cup | 250 mL |
| Lemon juice | 1 tbsp. | 15 mL |
| Poppy seeds | 1/3 cup | 75 mL |
| Finely grated lemon zest | 1 tbsp. | 15 mL |
| Butter (or hard margarine), softened | 1 cup | 250 mL |
| Granulated sugar | 1 cup | 250 mL |
| Icing (confectioner's) sugar | 1 cup | 250 mL |
| Egg yolks (large) | 3 | 3 |
| Vanilla | 1 tsp. | 5 mL |
| All-purpose flour | 2 cups | 500 mL |
| Baking soda | 1 tsp. | 5 mL |
| Salt | 1/2 tsp. | 2 mL |
| Egg whites (large), room temperature | 3 | 3 |

## LEMON BUTTERCREAM ICING

| | | |
|---|---|---|
| Granulated sugar | 1 cup | 250 mL |
| All-purpose flour | 1 1/2 tbsp. | 25 mL |
| Lemon juice | 3/4 cup | 175 mL |
| Egg yolks (large) | 6 | 6 |
| Butter (not margarine), cut into 8 pieces | 6 tbsp. | 100 mL |
| Finely grated lemon zest | 1 1/2 tbsp. | 25 mL |
| Whipping cream | 6 tbsp. | 100 mL |
| Butter (not margarine), softened | 2 2/3 cups | 650 mL |
| Icing (confectioner's) sugar | 2 1/4 cups | 550 mL |

**Poppy Seed Sheet Cake:** Grease 11 x 17 inch (28 x 43 cm) baking sheet. Line bottom with parchment (not waxed) paper, extending paper 2 inches (5 cm) over long sides (see page 12). Heat milk in small saucepan on medium for about 4 minutes until very hot and bubbles start to appear around edge.

Stir in lemon juice, poppy seeds and lemon zest. Let stand for about 15 minutes until cooled to room temperature.

Beat butter in large bowl until creamy and light coloured. Add both sugars. Beat well. Beat in egg yolks and vanilla.

Stir flour, baking soda and salt in medium bowl. Add to butter mixture in 3 parts, alternately with poppy seed mixture in 2 parts, beating well after each addition.

Beat egg whites in small bowl with clean beaters until stiff (not dry) peaks form. Do not overbeat. Gently fold 1/2 of egg white into poppy seed batter. Fold in remaining egg white until no white streaks remain. Spread evenly in prepared baking sheet. Bake in centre of 350°F (175°C) oven for about 20 minutes until wooden pick inserted in centre comes out clean. Let stand in baking sheet on wire rack until cooled completely. Run knife along sides to loosen. Invert cake onto counter. Carefully peel off and discard parchment paper. Trim off crusty edges all around. Cut cake crosswise into 3 rectangles, about 4 x 10 1/2 inches (10 x 26 cm) each.

**Lemon Buttercream Icing:** Combine granulated sugar and flour in medium saucepan. Whisk in lemon juice and egg yolks. Heat and whisk on medium for about 3 minutes until mixture is hot and sugar is dissolved.

Add first amount of butter, 1 piece at a time, stirring until melted. Heat and stir until just boiling and thickened. Whisk in lemon zest and whipping cream. Turn into medium bowl. Cover with plastic wrap directly on surface to prevent skin from forming. Chill until cold.

Beat second amount of butter in large bowl on high for about 5 minutes until light coloured and increased in volume.

Gradually add icing sugar, 1/4 cup (60 mL) at a time, beating well after each addition. Add lemon mixture, 1/4 cup (60 mL) at a time, beating until creamy and light coloured. Makes about 5 cups (1.25 L) icing. Place 1 cake piece on long 12 inch (30 cm) serving plate or cake board (see page 184). Spread 3/4 cup (175 mL) icing on top. Repeat with second and third cake pieces and same amount of icing each time. Place remaining cake piece on top. Ice top and sides with very thin layer of icing (see page 172). Spoon remaining icing into large piping bag fitted with small closed star tip. Pipe small stars on top and sides of cake (see page 175). Chill for several hours until firm for easier slicing. Cuts into 24 slices.

1 slice: 522 Calories; 37.2 g Total Fat (10.8 g Mono, 2.2 g Poly, 22 g Sat); 175 mg Cholesterol; 46 g Carbohydrate; trace Fibre; 4 g Protein; 453 mg Sodium

Pictured on page 35.

# German Chocolate Roll

*This dark chocolate cake comes together in a tight swirl. The filling and cake are one step in this easy and delicious roll.*

| | | |
|---|---|---|
| Butter (or hard margarine) | 1/4 cup | 60 mL |
| Brown sugar, packed | 1/4 cup | 60 mL |
| Whipping cream | 2 tbsp. | 30 mL |
| Can of sweetened condensed milk | 11 oz. | 300 mL |
| Egg yolks (large) | 2 | 2 |
| Flake coconut | 1/2 cup | 125 mL |
| Finely chopped pecans (or walnuts) | 1/2 cup | 125 mL |
| Vanilla | 1 tsp. | 5 mL |
| Large eggs | 3 | 3 |
| Granulated sugar | 1 cup | 250 mL |
| Vanilla | 1 tsp. | 5 mL |
| All-purpose flour | 2/3 cup | 150 mL |
| Cocoa, sifted if lumpy | 1/3 cup | 75 mL |
| Chocolate ice cream topping | 1/4 cup | 60 mL |
| Water | 2 tbsp. | 30 mL |
| Cocoa, sifted if lumpy | 3 tbsp. | 50 mL |
| Whipping cream | 7/8 cup | 200 mL |
| Icing (confectioner's) sugar | 2 tbsp. | 30 mL |
| Vanilla | 1/2 tsp. | 2 mL |

Frosted Flowers (page 181), for garnish

Line bottom of 10 × 15 inch (25 × 38 cm) jelly roll pan with parchment (not waxed) paper, extending paper 2 inches (5 cm) over long sides (see page 12). Melt butter in small saucepan. Add brown sugar and first amount whipping cream. Stir butter mixture on medium until sugar is dissolved. Remove from heat.

Stir in next 5 ingredients. Spread evenly in prepared pan.

Beat eggs in large bowl on high for about 6 minutes, adding granulated sugar, 1 tbsp. (15 mL) at a time, until thickened. Beat in second amount of vanilla.

Beat in flour, first amount of cocoa, ice cream topping and water on low until combined. Carefully spoon over coconut mixture. Spread evenly. Bake in 350°F (175°C) oven for 17 to 20 minutes until wooden pick inserted in centre comes out clean. Let stand in pan on wire rack for 5 minutes. Run knife along sides to loosen.

Spread large tea towel on counter. Cover with sheet of parchment (or waxed) paper. Sift second amount of cocoa evenly over paper. Invert cake onto cocoa. Carefully peel off and discard paper. Roll up from short end, using towel and paper as guide. Trim ends. Place roll, seam-side down, on long 12 inch (30 cm) serving plate or cake board (see page 184). Cool. Cuts into ten 1 inch (2.5 cm) slices.

Just before serving, beat second amount of whipping cream, icing sugar and third amount of vanilla in small bowl until soft peaks form. Spoon small dollop beside individual cake slices.

Garnish individual servings with Frosted Flowers. Serves 10.

1 serving: 525 Calories; 26.3 g Total Fat (8.9 g Mono, 2.3 g Poly, 13.4 g Sat); 164 mg Cholesterol; 68 g Carbohydrate; 2 g Fibre; 9 g Protein; 154 mg Sodium

Pictured on page 37.

# Chocolate Amaretti Layered Cake

*Only for those with a sweet tooth! The fresh strawberries in the topping go wonderfully with the decadent chocolate and subtle hint of liqueur in the cake.*

| | | |
|---|---|---|
| Package of amaretti cookies | 7 oz. | 200 g |
| Orange-flavoured liqueur (such as Grand Marnier) | 1/4 cup | 60 mL |

| | | |
|---|---|---|
| Dark chocolate bars (such as Lindt), 3 1/2 oz. (100 g) each, chopped | 5 | 5 |
| Butter (or hard margarine) | 1/2 cup | 125 mL |
| Egg yolks (large) | 2 | 2 |
| Whipping cream | 1 cup | 250 mL |
| Sliced fresh strawberries | 3 cups | 750 mL |
| Icing (confectioner's) sugar | 1/4 cup | 60 mL |

Grease 9 inch (22 cm) springform pan. Line bottom and side with parchment (not waxed) paper (see page 12). Process cookies in blender or food processor until coarse crumbs. Combine cookie crumbs and liqueur in medium bowl. Let stand for 10 minutes.

Heat chocolate and butter in heavy medium saucepan on lowest heat, stirring often, until chocolate is almost melted. Do not overheat. Remove from heat. Stir until smooth.

Stir in egg yolks, 1 at a time, stirring well after each addition. Cool.

Beat whipping cream in small bowl until soft peaks form. Fold into chocolate mixture. Pour 1/3 of whipped cream mixture into prepared pan. Carefully sprinkle with 1/2 of cookie mixture, patting crumbs down lightly. Spread with 1/2 of remaining whipped cream mixture. Sprinkle with remaining cookie mixture. Pat crumbs down lightly. Carefully spread remaining whipped cream mixture evenly over top. Cover. Chill for at least 6 hours or overnight until set. Remove from pan to serving plate.

Just before serving, scatter strawberries over top of cake. Dust liberally with icing sugar. Cuts into 10 wedges.

1 wedge: 670 Calories; 45.7 g Total Fat (13.4 g Mono, 1.7 g Poly, 28.2 g Sat); 123 mg Cholesterol; 67 g Carbohydrate; 5 g Fibre; 5 g Protein; 206 mg Sodium

Pictured below.

Top Left: Chocolate Amaretti Cake, page 36

Bottom Centre: German Chocolate Roll, page 36

# Coffee Liqueur Roll

*A sweet mocha icing fills and covers this roll. Fresh raspberries peek through the layers, adding a refreshing summer taste.*

| | | |
|---|---|---|
| Egg whites (large), room temperature | 4 | 4 |
| Granulated sugar | 2/3 cup | 150 mL |
| Egg yolks (large) | 4 | 4 |
| All-purpose flour | 1 cup | 250 mL |
| Baking powder | 2 tsp. | 10 mL |
| Instant coffee granules, crushed to fine powder | 1 1/2 tbsp. | 25 mL |
| Warm milk | 3 tbsp. | 50 mL |
| Vanilla | 1 tsp. | 5 mL |
| Granulated sugar | 1 tbsp. | 15 mL |
| **COFFEE FILLING** | | |
| Whipping cream | 1 1/2 cups | 375 mL |
| Icing (confectioner's) sugar | 1/4 cup | 60 mL |
| Coffee-flavoured liqueur (such as Kahlúa) | 3 tbsp. | 50 mL |
| Instant coffee granules, crushed to fine powder | 2 tsp. | 10 mL |
| Fresh raspberries | 1 1/2 cups | 375 mL |
| Fresh raspberries | 12 | 12 |
| Cocoa, sifted if lumpy | 2 tbsp. | 30 mL |

Chocolate Leaves, page 177, for decoration
Chocolate Filigrees, page 177, for decoration

Grease 10 x 15 inch (25 x 38 cm) jelly roll pan. Line bottom with parchment (not waxed) paper, extending paper 2 inches (5 cm) over long sides (see page 12). Beat egg whites in medium bowl until soft peaks form. Add first amount of sugar, 1 tbsp. (15 mL) at a time, beating well after each addition until sugar is dissolved.

Add egg yolks, 1 at a time, beating well after each addition until thick and light.

Fold in flour and baking powder.

Combine next 3 ingredients in small bowl. Fold into egg white mixture. Spread evenly in prepared pan. Bake in 375°F (190°C) oven for about 10 minutes until wooden pick inserted in centre comes out clean. Let stand in pan on wire rack for 5 minutes. Run knife along sides to loosen.

Spread large tea towel on counter. Cover with sheet of parchment (or waxed) paper. Sprinkle second amount of sugar over paper. Invert cake onto sugar. Carefully peel off and discard original parchment paper. Roll up cake from long side with towel. Let stand for about 10 minutes until cooled completely.

**Coffee Filling:** Beat whipping cream in medium bowl until soft peaks form. Add icing sugar. Beat until combined.

Combine liqueur and instant coffee in small cup. Fold into whipped cream mixture. Makes 3 cups (750 mL) filling. Unroll cake. Spread 1/2 of filling over cake to within 1 inch (2.5 cm) of each edge.

Sprinkle first amount of raspberries over filling. Roll up cake from long side, using towel and paper as guide. Trim ends. Place roll, seam-side down, on long 16 inch (40 cm) serving plate or cake board (see page 184). Spread with remaining filling. Cover loosely with plastic wrap. Chill until ready to serve.

Just before serving, place second amount of raspberries down centre of roll. Sprinkle cocoa over top.

Decorate with Chocolate Leaves and Filigrees (see page 177). Cuts into 12 slices.

1 slice: 251 Calories; 12.2 g Total Fat (3.7 g Mono, 0.7 g Poly, 7 g Sat); 109 mg Cholesterol; 30 g Carbohydrate; 1 g Fibre; 4 g Protein; 97 mg Sodium

Pictured on page 39.

Top: Brown Sugar Pecan Torte, page 40
Bottom: Coffee Liqueur Roll, this page

# Brown Sugar Pecan Torte

*This sweet, nutty torte has a unique hint of spices and liqueur. Layers are very rich so start with a small serving. Pecans are expensive . . . but this is well worth it!*

| | | |
|---|---|---|
| Egg yolks (large) | 6 | 6 |
| Brown sugar, packed | 1 cup | 250 mL |
| Milk (or half-and-half cream) | 1/4 cup | 60 mL |
| Brandy flavouring (or vanilla) | 1 tsp. | 5 mL |
| Pecan halves | 3 1/4 cups | 800 mL |
| All-purpose flour | 1/4 cup | 60 mL |
| Baking powder | 2 tsp. | 10 mL |
| Ground nutmeg | 1/4 tsp. | 1 mL |
| Salt | 1/4 tsp. | 1 mL |
| Egg whites (large), room temperature | 6 | 6 |
| Salt | 1/4 tsp. | 1 mL |
| Brown sugar, packed | 1 cup | 250 mL |
| Butter Ripple schnapps (or bourbon), optional | 1/4 cup | 60 mL |
| **BUTTER PECAN ICING** | | |
| Butter (not margarine), softened | 1 lb. | 454 g |
| Jars of marshmallow creme (7 oz., 198 g, each) | 3 | 3 |
| Pecan halves, toasted (see Tip, page 20) and coarsely chopped | 1 1/4 cups | 300 mL |

Grease 11 × 17 inch (28 × 43 cm) baking sheet. Line bottom with parchment (not waxed) paper, extending paper 2 inches (5 cm) over long sides (see page 12). Beat egg yolks and first amount of brown sugar in large bowl on high for about 5 minutes, scraping down side occasionally, until thick and creamy and doubled in volume.

Beat in milk and brandy flavouring.

Process next 5 ingredients in blender or food processor for 1 to 2 minutes. Pulse with on/off motion until pecans are finely ground. Add to egg yolk mixture. Mix well.

Beat egg whites and second amount of salt in separate large bowl with clean beaters until soft peaks form. Gradually add second amount of brown sugar, 1 tbsp. (15 mL) at a time, beating well after each addition until sugar is dissolved. Gently fold 1/2 of egg white mixture into pecan batter. Fold in remaining 1/2 of egg white mixture until no white streaks remain. Spread evenly in prepared baking sheet. Bake in centre of 350°F (175°C) oven for 30 to 35 minutes until wooden pick inserted in centre comes out clean. Let stand in baking sheet on wire rack until completely cooled. Run knife along sides to loosen. Turn cake out onto counter. Carefully peel off and discard parchment paper. Trim off crusty edges all around.

Brush surface of cake with schnapps. Cut cake crosswise into 4 rectangles, about 4 × 10 1/2 inches (10 × 26 cm) each.

**Butter Pecan Icing:** Beat butter in large bowl on high for about 5 minutes, scraping down side occasionally, until light coloured and increased in volume.

Add marshmallow creme, 1 spoonful at a time, beating on medium until smooth and fluffy.

Fold in 3/4 cup (175 mL) pecans. Makes 5 cups (1.25 L) icing. Divide and spread 3 cups (750 mL) icing on 3 cake pieces. Carefully stack pieces on top of each other as cake is very tender. Top with remaining cake piece. Spread top and sides with remaining icing. Sprinkle top with remaining pecans. Cover. Chill for at least 3 hours or up to 2 days. Cuts into fourteen 3/4 inch (2 cm) slices.

1 slice: 709 Calories; 46.6 g Total Fat (19.6 g Mono, 5.7 g Poly, 18.5 g Sat); 164 mg Cholesterol; 73 g Carbohydrate; 2 g Fibre; 6 g Protein; 468 mg Sodium

Pictured on page 39.

# Chocolate Pecan Upside-Down Cake

*Dense chocolate cake covered with a nutty caramel sauce. Garnish individual servings with a dollop of whipped cream or small scoop of ice cream.*

| | | |
|---|---|---|
| Butter (not margarine) | 3 tbsp. | 50 mL |
| Hard margarine (see Note) | 3 tbsp. | 50 mL |
| Brown sugar, packed | 1 cup | 250 mL |
| Water | 3 tbsp. | 50 mL |
| Pecan halves | 1 1/2 cups | 375 mL |

| | | |
|---|---|---|
| Butter (or hard margarine), softened | 1 cup | 250 mL |
| Granulated sugar | 1 cup | 250 mL |
| Vanilla | 1 tsp. | 5 mL |
| Large eggs | 3 | 3 |
| All-purpose flour | 1 1/4 cups | 300 mL |
| Cocoa, sifted if lumpy | 3/4 cup | 175 mL |
| Ground cinnamon | 1 tsp. | 5 mL |
| Baking powder | 3/4 tsp. | 4 mL |
| Baking soda | 1/4 tsp. | 1 mL |
| Salt | 1/4 tsp. | 1 mL |
| Sour cream | 1/2 cup | 125 mL |

Grease 9 inch (22 cm) springform pan. To prevent batter from leaking out of springform pan, use pan with a secure/tight-fitting base. Or set pan on sheet of foil and firmly press foil up around side of pan. Insert empty 14 oz. (398 mL) can filled 3/4 full with dried beans. Melt first amount of butter and margarine in medium saucepan on medium. Add brown sugar and water. Stir. Bring to a boil. Boil for about 3 minutes, stirring occasionally, until mixture is smooth and sauce-like (see page 16).

Coarsely chop 1/2 cup (125 mL) pecans. Add to brown sugar mixture. Add remaining pecans. Mix well. Turn into prepared pan. Press pecans down flat in single layer. Cool.

Beat second amount of butter, granulated sugar and vanilla in large bowl, scraping down side occasionally, until light and fluffy.

Add eggs, 1 at a time, beating well after each addition.

Combine next 6 ingredients in medium bowl.

Add flour mixture to butter mixture in 3 parts, alternately with sour cream in 2 parts, beating on low until combined. Carefully spoon batter into pan, spreading gently over pecan mixture in even layer. Bake in 350°F (175°C) oven for 45 to 50 minutes until wooden pick inserted near centre comes out clean. Let stand in pan on wire rack for 30 minutes. Run knife around inside and outside edges of cake. Remove can. Invert cake onto serving plate. Do not remove pan. Let stand inverted for 2 minutes. Remove pan and replace any pecans that have come off cake. Cool completely. Cuts into 12 pieces.

1 piece: 533 Calories; 35.6 g Total Fat (14.8 g Mono, 3.8 g Poly, 15.1 g Sat); 109 mg Cholesterol; 54 g Carbohydrate; 3 g Fibre; 6 g Protein; 358 mg Sodium

Pictured below.

**Note:** Although using all butter gives great flavour, the use of some margarine helps the caramel stay softer.

# Cheesecakes

The smooth, creamy textures in
this collection of recipes are partnered with
passionate flavours, such as tangy fruit and
rich chocolate. You'll want to savour every
last bite of these elegant desserts.

# Almond Pumpkin Cheesecake

*Who can resist a smooth, creamy cheesecake with an inviting spiced pumpkin flavour? The thick ginger cookie crust on the bottom is absolutely delightful!*

## ALMOND CRUST

| | | |
|---|---|---|
| Butter (or hard margarine) | 1/2 cup | 125 mL |
| Gingersnap crumbs (about 24 cookies, processed) | 2 cups | 500 mL |
| Sliced almonds, toasted (see Tip, page 20) | 1 cup | 250 mL |

## PUMPKIN FILLING

| | | |
|---|---|---|
| Blocks of cream cheese (8 oz., 250 g, each), softened | 2 | 2 |
| Granulated sugar | 3/4 cup | 175 mL |
| Brown sugar, packed | 1/4 cup | 60 mL |
| Large eggs | 4 | 4 |
| All-purpose flour | 1/4 cup | 60 mL |
| Ground ginger | 1/2 tsp. | 2 mL |
| Ground cinnamon | 1/4 tsp. | 1 mL |
| Ground nutmeg | 1/4 tsp. | 1 mL |
| Canned pure pumpkin (not filling) | 1 cup | 250 mL |
| Sour cream | 1 cup | 250 mL |
| Caramel ice cream topping | 1/2 cup | 125 mL |
| Chocolate ice cream topping | 2 tbsp. | 30 mL |
| Sliced almonds (with skins), toasted (see Tip, page 20) | 3/4 cup | 175 mL |

## MAPLE SHARDS (optional)

| | | |
|---|---|---|
| Maple (or maple-flavoured) syrup | 1 cup | 250 mL |
| Water | 1/2 cup | 125 mL |

**Almond Crust:** Lightly grease bottom and side of 9 inch (22 cm) springform pan. Melt butter in medium saucepan. Remove from heat. Add crumbs and almonds. Mix well. Press evenly in bottom of prepared pan with flat-bottomed glass. Chill for 1 hour.

**Pumpkin Filling:** Beat cream cheese, granulated sugar and brown sugar in large bowl until smooth. Add eggs, 1 at a time, beating until just combined.

Add next 6 ingredients. Mix. Pour filling onto crust. Spread evenly. Bake in 325°F (160°C) oven for about 1 1/4 hours until almost set. Filling may still wobble in middle, but will set upon cooling. Immediately run knife around inside edge of pan to allow cheesecake to settle evenly. Cool completely.

Cover. Chill for at least 6 hours or overnight.

Spread caramel topping evenly over top of cheesecake. Drizzle chocolate topping in long loops, about 1 inch (2.5 cm) apart, over caramel topping.

Gently drag wooden pick or skewer through lines to create marble effect.

Sprinkle almonds around top edge.

**Maple Shards:** Combine maple syrup and water to make a sugar mixture (see page 16). Use mixture to make shards (see page 180). Set shards randomly into centre of cheesecake. Serve immediately. Cuts into 12 wedges.

1 wedge: 584 Calories; 38.1 g Total Fat (14.6 g Mono, 3.4 g Poly, 17.9 g Sat); 148 mg Cholesterol; 54 g Carbohydrate; 3 g Fibre; 11 g Protein; 421 mg Sodium

Pictured on front cover.

# White Chocolate Mousse Cake

*This smooth, light cheesecake has a refreshing, summery flavour. The pink polka dots throughout the ivory-coloured filling is pretty and fun.*

### VANILLA CRUST

| | | |
|---|---|---|
| Butter (or hard margarine) | 1/3 cup | 75 mL |
| Vanilla wafer crumbs (about 2 cups, 500 mL, wafers, processed) | 1 1/4 cups | 300 mL |

### WHITE CHOCOLATE FILLING

| | | |
|---|---|---|
| Envelope of unflavoured gelatin (equivalent to 1 tbsp., 15 mL) | 1 | 1 |
| Water | 1/3 cup | 75 mL |
| Block of cream cheese, softened | 8 oz. | 250 g |
| Granulated sugar | 1/2 cup | 125 mL |
| White chocolate bar, melted | 6 oz. | 170 g |
| Egg whites (large), room temperature | 2 | 2 |
| Whipping cream | 1 cup | 250 mL |
| Strawberry ice cream topping, large pieces chopped | 1/3 cup | 75 mL |
| Drops of red food colouring | 1 – 2 | 1 – 2 |

### STRAWBERRY TOPPING

| | | |
|---|---|---|
| Fresh medium strawberries, hulled and halved lengthwise (see Note) | 26 | 26 |
| Unflavoured gelatin | 1 tsp. | 5 mL |
| Cranberry cocktail | 1/2 cup | 125 mL |
| Grenadine syrup | 2 tbsp. | 30 mL |

**Vanilla Crust:** Melt butter in medium saucepan. Remove from heat. Add crumbs. Mix well. Press evenly in bottom of ungreased 9 inch (22 cm) springform pan with flat-bottomed glass. Chill for 1 hour.

**White Chocolate Filling:** Sprinkle gelatin over water in small saucepan. Let stand for 1 minute. Heat and stir on low until dissolved completely. Cool slightly.

Beat cream cheese and sugar in large bowl until smooth. Add chocolate. Beat well. Add gelatin mixture. Beat well.

Beat egg whites with clean beaters in medium bowl until soft peaks form. Fold into cream cheese mixture in 2 batches.

Beat whipping cream in separate medium bowl until soft peaks form. Fold into cream cheese mixture. Makes 3 3/4 cups (925 mL) filling. Reserve 1 1/2 cups (375 mL). Spoon remaining filling onto crust. Spread evenly.

Add strawberry ice cream topping and food colouring to reserved filling. Mix well. Spoon into piping bag fitted with 1/3 inch (1 cm) plain tip (see page 15). Poke tip into filling in pan. Squeeze bag gently to squirt some filling into cheesecake. Repeat randomly all over until all strawberry mixture is used. Cover. Chill for at least 6 hours or overnight.

**Strawberry Topping:** Arrange strawberry halves, cut side down, in single layer on cheesecake, leaving cheesecake in pan.

Sprinkle gelatin over cranberry cocktail and grenadine in small saucepan. Let stand for 1 minute. Heat and stir on low until dissolved completely. Cool. Stir. Carefully pour over strawberries to cover completely. Chill for at least 3 hours until firm. Remove from pan onto serving plate. Cuts into 12 wedges.

1 wedge: 413 Calories; 26 g Total Fat (7.8 g Mono, 1.4 g Poly, 15.1 g Sat); 73 mg Cholesterol; 42 g Carbohydrate; 1 g Fibre; 5 g Protein; 196 mg Sodium

Pictured on page 45.

**Note:** Leave the hulls on some of the strawberries to arrange around outer edge and centre of cake.

# Ginger Cookie Cheesecake

*This would make a wonderful Christmastime cheesecake with its warm spice and eggnog flavour. The texture is light and fluffy.*

### GINGER NUT CRUST

| | | |
|---|---|---|
| Butter (or hard margarine) | 1/3 cup | 75 mL |
| Gingersnap crumbs (about 17 cookies, processed) | 1 1/2 cups | 375 mL |
| Pecans, finely chopped | 1/2 cup | 125 mL |

### EGGNOG FILLING

| | | |
|---|---|---|
| Envelope of unflavoured gelatin (equivalent to 1 tbsp., 15 mL) | 1 | 1 |
| Dark rum | 3 tbsp. | 50 mL |
| Blocks of cream cheese (8 oz., 250 g, each), softened | 2 | 2 |
| Milk | 1 cup | 250 mL |
| Eggnog | 2 cups | 500 mL |
| Instant vanilla pudding powder (4 serving size), reserve 1 tbsp. (15 mL) powder | 1 | 1 |
| Ground cinnamon | 1/4 tsp. | 1 mL |
| Ground nutmeg | 1/4 tsp. | 1 mL |
| Whipping cream | 1 cup | 250 mL |
| Gold sugar sprinkles | 1/4 cup | 60 mL |

### NUTMEG ROLLS (optional)

| | | |
|---|---|---|
| Egg whites (large), room temperature | 2 | 2 |
| Brown sugar, packed | 6 tbsp. | 100 mL |
| Salt, just a pinch | | |
| Vanilla | 1/4 tsp. | 1 mL |
| Butter (or hard margarine), melted | 1/4 cup | 60 mL |
| All-purpose flour | 1/2 cup | 125 mL |
| Ground nutmeg | 1/2 tsp. | 2 mL |

### TOPPING

| | | |
|---|---|---|
| Whipping cream | 1/2 cup | 125 mL |
| Reserved instant vanilla pudding powder | 1 tbsp. | 15 mL |

Ground nutmeg (or cinnamon), just a sprinkle

Gold sugar sprinkles, for garnish

**Ginger Nut Crust:** Melt butter in medium saucepan. Remove from heat. Add crumbs and pecans. Mix well. Press evenly in bottom of ungreased 9 inch (22 cm) springform pan with flat-bottomed glass. Bake in 350°F (175°C) oven for 10 minutes. Let stand on wire rack to cool.

**Eggnog Filling:** Sprinkle gelatin over rum in small saucepan. Let stand for 1 minute. Heat and stir on low until dissolved completely. Cool slightly.

Beat cream cheese and milk in large bowl until smooth. Add eggnog, pudding powder, cinnamon and nutmeg. Beat well. Add gelatin mixture. Mix.

Beat whipping cream in medium bowl until soft peaks form. Fold into eggnog mixture. Pour onto crust. Spread evenly. Cover. Chill for at least 4 hours until firm. Remove side of pan.

Sprinkle top of cheesecake with sugar sprinkles.

**Nutmeg Rolls** (see page 178): Line bottom of baking sheet with parchment (not waxed) paper. Trace 5 circles, 2 3/4 inches (7 cm) in diameter and about 1 inch (2.5 cm) apart, on paper. Turn paper over. Beat first 4 ingredients in medium bowl until frothy.

Beat in butter.

Add flour and nutmeg. Whisk until no lumps remain. Measure 1 tsp. (5 mL) batter onto each circle. Spread evenly with offset spatula to fill circles. Bake in 350°F (175°C) oven for 5 to 6 minutes until lightly browned (see Note).

Working quickly, pick up 1 cookie with spatula. Place over pencil or wooden spoon handle. Roll around pencil to form tight cylinder. Repeat with remaining cookies. Let stand for 3 to 4 minutes until set and cooled before removing. Cookies on baking sheet may be warmed in oven to soften if they become too hard. Repeat with remaining batter, making 5 rolls at a time (see Note). Makes about 44 rolls, enough to surround 9 inch (22 cm) round dessert.

Arrange rolls upright around cheesecake. Wrap with thin ribbon if desired.

**Topping:** Beat whipping cream with reserved pudding powder in medium bowl until stiff. Spoon into piping bag fitted with medium open star tip. Pipe 12 rosettes around edge of cheesecake (see page 175).

Sprinkle each rosette with pinch of nutmeg and sugar sprinkles. Cuts into 12 wedges.

1 wedge: 512 Calories; 39 g Total Fat (12.9 g Mono, 2.3 g Poly, 21.6 g Sat); 124 mg Cholesterol; 32 g Carbohydrate; 1 g Fibre; 8 g Protein; 471 mg Sodium

Pictured below.

**Note:** Having 2 baking sheets and 2 pieces of parchment paper with drawn circles helps this process go much faster. As soon as you remove cookies from the oven, put the other baking sheet in to bake while you form the rolls and then get another batch ready on the parchment paper.

# Black Currant Cheesecake

*The attractive plum-coloured swirls add colour and a touch of flavour to the golden cheesecake. The shortbread crust has a wonderful, citrus undertone. If large cracks appear in the top of the cake after baking, pipe sweetened whipped cream over the cheesecake to cover.*

## CRUST

| | | |
|---|---|---|
| Butter (or hard margarine), softened | 3/4 cup | 175 mL |
| Granulated sugar | 1/3 cup | 75 mL |
| Finely grated lemon zest | 1 tsp. | 5 mL |
| All-purpose flour | 1 2/3 cups | 400 mL |
| Cornstarch | 1/4 cup | 60 mL |
| Salt | 1/4 tsp. | 1 mL |

## FILLING

| | | |
|---|---|---|
| Blocks of cream cheese (8 oz., 250 g, each), softened | 2 | 2 |
| Granulated sugar | 1/2 cup | 125 mL |
| Egg yolks (large) | 4 | 4 |
| Sour cream | 1 cup | 250 mL |
| Vanilla | 1 1/2 tsp. | 7 mL |
| Egg whites (large), room temperature | 4 | 4 |
| Black currant jam | 1/2 cup | 125 mL |
| All-purpose flour | 1 tbsp. | 15 mL |

**Crust:** Beat butter, sugar and lemon zest in medium bowl until light and fluffy.

Combine flour, cornstarch and salt in small bowl. Add to butter mixture. Mix well. Press evenly in bottom and 1 inch (2.5 cm) up side of ungreased 10 inch (25 cm) springform pan with flat-bottomed glass. Bake in 350°F (175°C) oven for about 25 minutes until slightly puffed and golden. Let stand on wire rack to cool.

**Filling:** Beat cream cheese and sugar in large bowl until smooth. Add egg yolks, sour cream and vanilla. Beat on low until just combined.

Beat egg whites with clean beaters in medium bowl on high until stiff (not dry) peaks form. Fold into cream cheese mixture. Makes about 6 cups (1.5 L) filling. Pour 3 cups (750 mL) filling into crust.

Put jam and flour into small bowl. Stir until blended. Fold 1/2 cup (125 mL) filling into jam mixture.

Spoon 1/2 cup (125 mL) jam mixture in small dabs over filling in pan. Cover with remaining filling and jam mixture in small dabs.

Cut through mixtures with blunt knife in swirling motion to create marble effect. Bake in 325°F (160°C) oven for about 1 1/4 hours until filling is almost set. Filling may still wobble in middle, but will set upon cooling. Immediately run knife around inside edge of pan to allow cheesecake to settle evenly. Cool completely. Cover. Chill for at least 6 hours or overnight. Cuts into 12 wedges.

1 wedge: 481 Calories; 31.4 g Total Fat (9.1 g Mono, 1.4 g Poly, 19.1 g Sat); 158 mg Cholesterol; 43 g Carbohydrate; 1 g Fibre; 8 g Protein; 333 mg Sodium

Pictured on page 50.

# Mango Swirl Cheesecake

*You'll love the tropical flavours in this fresh, light cheesecake. The coconut crust is a taste sensation.*

## COCONUT CRUST

|  | | |
|---|---|---|
| Butter (or hard margarine) | 2/3 cup | 150 mL |
| Graham cracker crumbs | 1 3/4 cups | 425 mL |
| Long thread coconut | 2/3 cup | 150 mL |

## COCONUT FILLING

|  | | |
|---|---|---|
| Envelope of unflavoured gelatin (equivalent to 1 tbsp., 15 mL) | 1 | 1 |
| Water | 2 tbsp. | 30 mL |
| Block of cream cheese, softened | 8 oz. | 250 g |
| Coconut milk | 1 cup | 250 mL |
| Granulated sugar | 1/2 cup | 125 mL |

## MANGO FILLING

|  | | |
|---|---|---|
| Envelope of unflavoured gelatin (equivalent to 1 tbsp., 15 mL) | 1 | 1 |
| Water | 2 tbsp. | 30 mL |
| Block of cream cheese, softened | 8 oz. | 250 g |
| Can of sliced mango, drained and puréed | 14 oz. | 398 mL |
| Granulated sugar | 1/2 cup | 125 mL |
| Drops of yellow food colouring | 2 | 2 |
| Drop of red food colouring | 1 | 1 |

**Coconut Crust:** Lightly grease bottom and side of 9 inch (22 cm) springform pan. Melt butter in medium saucepan. Remove from heat. Add graham crumbs and coconut. Stir. Press evenly in bottom and 1 inch (2.5 cm) up side of prepared pan with flat-bottomed glass. Chill for 1 hour.

**Coconut Filling:** Sprinkle gelatin over water in small saucepan. Let stand for 1 minute. Heat and stir on low until dissolved completely. Cool slightly.

Beat next 3 ingredients in large bowl until smooth. Add gelatin mixture. Stir.

**Mango Filling:** Sprinkle gelatin over water in small saucepan. Let stand for 1 minute. Heat and stir on low until dissolved completely. Cool.

Beat cream cheese, mango and sugar in large bowl until smooth. Stir in gelatin mixture and food colouring. Mix well. Randomly dollop mango mixture and coconut mixture into prepared crust. Cut through mixtures with blunt knife in swirling motion to create marble effect. Cover. Chill for at least 6 hours or overnight. Cuts into 12 wedges.

1 wedge: 442 Calories; 32.4 g Total Fat (8.1 g Mono, 1.2 g Poly, 21.2 g Sat); 75 mg Cholesterol; 35 g Carbohydrate; 1 g Fibre; 6 g Protein; 328 mg Sodium

Pictured on page 51.

Cheesecakes freeze well. It is important to completely cool cheesecake before storing to prevent condensation from forming and spoiling appearance. Wrap cake securely in double layer of plastic wrap, then in heavy-duty foil. Do not add garnishes or toppings before freezing. Store in freezer for up to 1 month. To thaw, place wrapped cheesecake in refrigerator overnight.

**Photo Legend next page:**
Left: Black Currant Cheesecake, page 48
Right: Mango Swirl Cheesecake, this page

# Caramel Apple Cheesecake

*This high cheesecake has a creamy topping that complements the tart apple filling perfectly. Double the sauce to drizzle on individual plates for an elegant presentation.*

### PECAN CRUST

| | | |
|---|---|---|
| Butter (or hard margarine) | 2/3 cup | 150 mL |
| Vanilla wafer crumbs (about 4 cups, 1 L, wafers, processed) | 2 cups | 500 mL |
| Pecans, toasted (see Tip, page 20) and finely ground in blender | 1 cup | 250 mL |

### APPLE FILLING

| | | |
|---|---|---|
| Cooking oil | 1 tbsp. | 15 mL |
| Butter (or hard margarine) | 1 tbsp. | 15 mL |
| Peeled and chopped tart cooking apple (such as Granny Smith) | 3 cups | 750 mL |
| Brown sugar, packed | 1/4 cup | 60 mL |
| Unflavoured gelatin | 4 tsp. | 20 mL |
| Apple juice | 1/3 cup | 75 mL |
| Blocks of cream cheese (8 oz., 250 g, each), softened | 2 | 2 |
| Sour cream | 1 cup | 250 mL |
| Granulated sugar | 2/3 cup | 150 mL |
| Ground cinnamon | 1/2 tsp. | 2 mL |
| Whipping cream | 1 cup | 250 mL |
| Pecan halves, toasted (see Tip, page 20) | 24 | 24 |

### CARAMEL SAUCE

| | | |
|---|---|---|
| Butter (or hard margarine) | 2 tbsp. | 30 mL |
| Whipping cream | 2 tbsp. | 30 mL |
| Brown sugar, packed | 2 tbsp. | 30 mL |
| Large white marshmallows, quartered | 4 | 4 |

**Pecan Crust:** Melt butter in large saucepan. Remove from heat. Add crumbs and pecans. Stir. Press evenly in bottom and 2/3 up side of ungreased 9 inch (22 cm) springform pan with flat-bottomed glass. Chill for 1 hour.

**Apple Filling:** Heat cooking oil and butter in large frying pan on medium. Add apple. Cook for about 10 minutes, stirring occasionally, until apple is softened.

Add brown sugar. Heat and stir until sugar is dissolved. Simmer, stirring occasionally, for about 5 minutes until thickened. Turn into medium bowl. Cool completely.

Sprinkle gelatin over apple juice in small saucepan. Let stand for 1 minute. Heat and stir on low until dissolved completely. Cool slightly.

Put next 4 ingredients into large bowl. Beat well. Add gelatin mixture. Beat. Add apple mixture. Stir.

Beat whipping cream in same medium bowl until soft peaks form. Fold into cream cheese mixture. Pour into crust. Spread evenly.

Arrange pecan halves around outside edge of cheesecake. Cover. Chill for at least 6 hours or overnight.

**Caramel Sauce:** Put all 4 ingredients into medium saucepan. Heat and stir on medium until marshmallow is melted and brown sugar is dissolved. Cool slightly. Makes 1/4 cup (60 mL) sauce. Pour onto centre of cheesecake. Spread sauce just to edge of pecans. Chill for at least 1 hour until sauce is completely set. Cuts into 12 wedges.

1 wedge: 669 Calories; 52.5 g Total Fat (18.9 g Mono, 4.9 g Poly, 25.8 g Sat); 130 mg Cholesterol; 47 g Carbohydrate; 1 g Fibre; 7 g Protein; 352 mg Sodium

Pictured on page 53.

*Cheesecakes*

# Fruit 'N' Chocolate Cheesecake

*A creamy chocolate dessert with a melt-in-your-mouth filling.*

**CHOCOLATE CRUST**

| | | |
|---|---|---|
| Butter (or hard margarine) | 1/3 cup | 75 mL |
| Chocolate wafer crumbs | 2 cups | 500 mL |

**FILLING**

| | | |
|---|---|---|
| Envelope of unflavoured gelatin (equivalent to 1 tbsp., 15 mL) | 1 | 1 |
| Coffee-flavoured liqueur (such as Kahlúa) | 1/4 cup | 60 mL |
| Ricotta cheese | 2 cups | 500 mL |
| Icing (confectioner's) sugar | 1 cup | 250 mL |
| Grated semi-sweet chocolate baking squares (about 2), chilled before and after grating see page 177 | 1/2 cup | 125 mL |
| Red glazed cherries, coarsely chopped | 1/4 cup | 60 mL |
| Glazed pineapple rings, diced (about 1/3 cup, 75 mL) | 2 | 2 |

**TOPPING**

| | | |
|---|---|---|
| Whipping cream | 1/2 cup | 125 mL |
| Grated semi-sweet chocolate (about 1 1/2 baking squares) | 1/3 cup | 75 mL |

**Chocolate Crust:** Melt butter in medium saucepan. Remove from heat. Add wafer crumbs. Stir. Press evenly in bottom and 1/2 inch (12 mm) up side of ungreased 8 inch (20 cm) springform pan with flat-bottomed glass. Chill for 1 hour.

**Filling:** Sprinkle gelatin over liqueur in small saucepan. Let stand for 1 minute. Heat and stir on low until dissolved completely. Cool slightly.

Beat cheese and icing sugar in large bowl on high until well combined. Add gelatin mixture. Beat.

Add next 3 ingredients. Stir. Spoon cheese mixture into crust. Spread evenly. Chill for at least 6 hours or overnight.

**Topping:** Beat whipping cream in small bowl until soft peaks form. Spread evenly over top of cheesecake.

Sprinkle with chocolate. Cuts into 12 wedges.

1 wedge: 335 Calories; 15.9 g Total Fat (5.3 g Mono, 0.8 g Poly, 8.9 g Sat); 36 mg Cholesterol; 41 g Carbohydrate; trace Fibre; 7 g Protein; 207 mg Sodium

Pictured on page 55.

# Ricotta Pine Nut Cheesecake

*Coffee lovers can indulge in the warm flavours of nutmeg, Kahlúa and coffee with this sweet cheesecake.*

**CRUST**

| | | |
|---|---|---|
| All-purpose flour | 1 3/4 cups | 425 mL |
| Baking powder | 2 tsp. | 10 mL |
| Ground almonds | 1/2 cup | 125 mL |
| Cold butter (or hard margarine), cut up | 2/3 cup | 150 mL |
| Granulated sugar | 1/2 cup | 125 mL |
| Ice water, approximately | 1 tbsp. | 15 mL |

**FILLING**

| | | |
|---|---|---|
| Ricotta cheese | 2 1/4 lbs. | 1 kg |
| Granulated sugar | 1 cup | 250 mL |
| Egg yolks (large) | 2 | 2 |
| Pine nuts, toasted (see Tip, page 20) | 1/2 cup | 125 mL |
| Finely chopped dried apricots | 1/2 cup | 125 mL |
| Semi-sweet chocolate baking squares (1 oz., 28 g, each), chopped | 3 | 3 |
| All-purpose flour | 2 tbsp. | 30 mL |
| Ground nutmeg | 1/2 tsp. | 2 mL |
| Coffee-flavoured liqueur (such as Kahlúa) | 3 tbsp. | 50 mL |

## COFFEE SAUCE (optional)

| | | |
|---|---|---|
| Whipping cream | 1/2 cup | 125 mL |
| Brown sugar, packed | 1/2 cup | 125 mL |
| Prepared strong coffee | 1/3 cup | 75 mL |

**Crust:** Combine first 3 ingredients in large bowl. Cut in butter until mixture resembles coarse crumbs.

Add sugar. Stir.

Work in enough ice water until soft dough forms. Roll pastry out onto lightly floured surface to 1/8 inch (3 mm) thickness. Line bottom and 1 inch (2.5 cm) up side of ungreased 10 inch (25 cm) springform pan with pastry. Cover. Chill for 1 hour.

**Filling:** Beat first 3 ingredients in large bowl until just combined.

Add next 6 ingredients. Mix. Spoon mixture into pastry shell. Spread evenly. Bake in 350°F (175°C) oven for about 1 1/4 hours until almost set. Filling may still wobble in middle, but will set upon cooling. Immediately run knife around inside edge of pan to allow cheesecake to settle evenly. Cool completely. Cover. Chill for at least 6 hours or overnight.

**Coffee Sauce:** Combine all 3 ingredients in medium saucepan. Heat and stir on low until brown sugar is dissolved. Bring to a boil on medium. Boil gently for 5 to 10 minutes until sauce is thickened. Makes about 3/4 cup (175 mL) sauce. Serve with cheesecake. Cuts into 12 wedges.

1 wedge: 545 Calories; 30 g Total Fat (9.6 g Mono, 2.8 g Poly, 16 g Sat); 107 mg Cholesterol; 57 g Carbohydrate; 3 g Fibre; 15 g Protein; 246 mg Sodium

Pictured below.

Top: Ricotta Pine Nut Cheesecake, page 54
Bottom: Fruit 'N' Chocolate Cheesecake, page 54

# Irish Cheesecake

*If you enjoy the taste of Irish cream liqueur,
you will love this dessert.*

**VANILLA CRUST**

| | | |
|---|---|---|
| Butter (or hard margarine) | 1/3 cup | 75 mL |
| Vanilla wafer crumbs (about 2 cups, 500 mL, wafers, processed) | 1 1/4 cups | 300 mL |

**FILLING**

| | | |
|---|---|---|
| Blocks of cream cheese (8 oz., 250 g, each), softened | 2 | 2 |
| Granulated sugar | 1/2 cup | 125 mL |
| Large eggs | 3 | 3 |
| Sour cream | 1 cup | 250 mL |
| All-purpose flour | 2 tbsp. | 30 mL |
| Irish cream-flavoured liqueur (such as Baileys Irish Cream) | 3/4 cup | 175 mL |

Chocolate Curls, page 177, for garnish
Shaved chocolate, page 177, for garnish
Cocoa, for dusting

**Vanilla Crust:** Grease 9 inch (22 cm) springform pan. Melt butter in medium saucepan. Remove from heat. Add crumbs. Mix well. Press evenly in bottom of prepared pan with flat-bottomed glass. Chill for 1 hour.

**Filling:** Beat cream cheese and sugar in large bowl until smooth. Add eggs, 1 at a time, beating until just combined.

Add sour cream. Beat until just combined.

Add flour and liqueur. Stir well. Pour cream cheese mixture onto crust. Spread evenly. Place pan on large piece of heavy-duty foil. Bring foil up around pan. Press firmly around base and side of pan, ensuring foil comes up 1 inch (2.5 cm) higher than side. Secure with string. Place in casserole or roaster. Carefully pour enough hot water into casserole to come halfway up side of springform pan. Bake in 325°F (160°C) oven for 55 to 60 minutes until almost set. Filling may still wobble in middle, but will set upon cooling. Immediately run knife around inside edge of pan to allow cheesecake to settle evenly. Cool completely. Cover. Chill for at least 6 hours or overnight.

Arrange Chocolate Curls around top outer edge of cheesecake. Sprinkle centre with shaved chocolate. Dust with cocoa. Cuts into 12 wedges.

1 wedge: 397 Calories; 28.7 g Total Fat (8.5 g Mono, 1.6 g Poly, 16.7 g Sat); 133 mg Cholesterol; 26 g Carbohydrate; trace Fibre; 7 g Protein; 262 mg Sodium

Pictured on page 57.

Bottom Left: Cappuccino Cheesecake, page 58
Top Right: Irish Cheesecake, above

# Cappuccino Cheesecake

*This palate-pleasing cheesecake is a velvety smooth blend of coffee and liqueur flavours. The truffles create a special presentation, but if you don't have time, the cheesecake is luscious by itself.*

### CHOCOLATE CRUST

| | | |
|---|---|---|
| Butter (or hard margarine) | 2/3 cup | 150 mL |
| Chocolate wafer crumbs | 3 cups | 750 mL |

### COFFEE FILLING

| | | |
|---|---|---|
| Unflavoured gelatin | 4 tsp. | 20 mL |
| Prepared strong coffee, cooled | 2/3 cup | 150 mL |
| Blocks of cream cheese (8 oz., 250 g, each), softened | 2 | 2 |
| Sour cream | 1/2 cup | 125 mL |
| Granulated sugar | 3/4 cup | 175 mL |
| Whipping cream | 1 cup | 250 mL |
| Cocoa, for dusting | | |

### COFFEE TRUFFLES (optional)

| | | |
|---|---|---|
| Whipping cream | 1 1/2 tbsp. | 25 mL |
| Butter (or hard margarine) | 1 1/2 tbsp. | 25 mL |
| Semi-sweet chocolate baking squares (1 oz., 28 g, each), chopped | 6 | 6 |
| Coffee-flavoured liqueur (such as Kahlúa) | 1 tbsp. | 15 mL |
| White chocolate melting wafers (about 4 oz., 113 g) | 1 cup | 250 mL |
| Cocoa, for dusting | | |

**Chocolate Crust:** Melt butter in medium saucepan. Remove from heat. Add wafer crumbs. Mix well. Press evenly in bottom and 1 inch (2.5 cm) up side of ungreased 9 inch (22 cm) springform pan with flat-bottomed glass. Chill for 1 hour.

**Coffee Filling:** Sprinkle gelatin over coffee in small saucepan. Let stand for 1 minute. Heat and stir on low until dissolved completely. Cool slightly.

Beat cream cheese, sour cream and sugar in large bowl until smooth and well combined. Add gelatin mixture. Beat.

Beat whipping cream in small bowl until soft peaks form. Fold into cream cheese mixture. Spoon into crust. Spread evenly. Cover. Chill for at least 8 hours or overnight.

Dust top of cheesecake with cocoa.

**Coffee Truffles:** Combine first 3 ingredients in small heavy saucepan. Heat and stir on lowest heat, stirring often, until chocolate is almost melted. Do not overheat. Remove from heat. Stir until smooth.

Add liqueur. Stir. Turn into small bowl. Chill for about 2 hours until firm. Roll into balls using 1 tsp. (5 mL) for each. Place on foil-lined baking sheet. Chill for about 1 hour until firm.

Heat melting wafers in small heavy saucepan on lowest heat for about 3 minutes, stirring often, until almost melted (see page 17). Do not overheat. Remove from heat. Stir until smooth. Dip balls into white chocolate. Place, not touching, on baking sheet. Cool until chocolate is set.

Arrange truffles around outer edge of cheesecake. Dust truffles lightly with cocoa. Cuts into 12 wedges.

1 wedge: 503 Calories; 37.7 g Total Fat (11.9 g Mono, 1.7 g Poly, 22.1 g Sat); 104 mg Cholesterol; 37 g Carbohydrate; 0 g Fibre; 7 g Protein; 420 mg Sodium

Pictured on page 56/57.

# Rum Raisin Cheesecake

*This sinfully delicious cheesecake combines the flavours of rum, raisins and chocolate. Add a dollop of whipped cream and shaved chocolate (see page 177) to create a finished look.*

### CRUST

| | | |
|---|---|---|
| Butter (or hard margarine) | 1/3 cup | 75 mL |
| Chocolate chip cookie crumbs (about 16 cookies, processed) | 1 1/2 cups | 375 mL |

### FILLING

| | | |
|---|---|---|
| Dark raisins | 1 cup | 250 mL |
| Spiced rum | 2/3 cup | 150 mL |
| Blocks of cream cheese (8 oz., 250 g, each), softened | 2 | 2 |
| Granulated sugar | 1/2 cup | 125 mL |
| Large eggs | 4 | 4 |

| | | |
|---|---|---|
| Milk chocolate bars (3 1/2 oz., 100 g, each), melted | 2 | 2 |
| Sour cream | 1 cup | 250 mL |
| All-purpose flour | 3 tbsp. | 50 mL |

Cocoa, for dusting

**Crust:** Grease bottom and side of 9 inch (22 cm) springform pan. Melt butter in medium saucepan. Remove from heat. Add crumbs. Mix well. Press evenly in bottom of prepared pan with flat-bottomed glass. Chill for 1 hour.

**Filling:** Combine raisins and rum in small bowl. Let stand for 1 hour. Do not drain.

Beat cream cheese and sugar in large bowl until smooth. Add eggs, 1 at a time, beating until just combined.

Add next 3 ingredients. Add raisin mixture. Stir. Pour onto crust. Spread evenly. Bake in 325°F (160°C) oven for about 1 hour until almost set. Filling may still wobble in middle, but will set upon cooling. Immediately run knife around inside edge of pan to allow cheesecake to settle evenly. Cool completely. Cover. Chill for at least 6 hours or overnight.

Dust cheesecake with cocoa. Cuts into 12 wedges.

1 wedge: 529 Calories; 32.5 g Total Fat (10.3 g Mono, 1.6 g Poly, 18.7 g Sat); 144 mg Cholesterol; 46 g Carbohydrate; 1 g Fibre; 9 g Protein; 294 mg Sodium

Pictured below.

Rum Raisin Cheesecake, page 58

# Upside-Down Cheesecakes

*The golden crumb crust is on top of these individual cheesecakes.*

### HAZELNUT CRUST

| | | |
|---|---|---|
| Butter (or hard margarine) | 1/3 cup | 75 mL |
| Vanilla wafer crumbs (about 2 cups, 500 mL, wafers, processed) | 1 1/4 cups | 300 mL |
| Hazelnuts (filberts), toasted (see Tip, page 20) and finely ground in blender | 1 cup | 250 mL |

### WHITE CHOCOLATE FILLING

| | | |
|---|---|---|
| Envelope of unflavoured gelatin (equivalent to 1 tbsp., 15 mL) | 1 | 1 |
| Water | 1/3 cup | 75 mL |
| Block of cream cheese, softened | 8 oz. | 250 g |
| Sour cream | 1 cup | 250 mL |
| Granulated sugar | 1/3 cup | 75 mL |
| White chocolate baking squares (1 oz., 28 g, each), melted | 6 | 6 |
| Hazelnut-flavoured liqueur (such as Frangelico) | 3 tbsp. | 50 mL |
| Whipping cream | 1/2 cup | 125 mL |

### CHOCOLATE SAUCE

| | | |
|---|---|---|
| Semi-sweet chocolate baking squares (1 oz., 28 g, each), chopped | 4 | 4 |
| Whipping cream | 1/4 cup | 60 mL |
| Butter (or hard margarine) | 1 tbsp. | 15 mL |
| Hazelnut-flavoured liqueur (such as Frangelico) | 1 tbsp. | 15 mL |
| Chocolate Filigrees, page 177 (optional) | 6 | 6 |

**Hazelnut Crust:** Grease six 1 cup (250 mL) metal molds or ramekins with straight sides, about 3 1/2 to 3 3/4 inches (9 to 9.5 cm) in diameter. Cut circles of parchment (or waxed) paper large enough to fit into bottom of each mold. Line sides with parchment (or waxed) paper.

Melt butter in medium saucepan. Remove from heat. Add crumbs and hazelnuts. Stir. Press evenly into each mold with flat-bottomed glass. Chill for 15 minutes.

**White Chocolate Filling:** Sprinkle gelatin over water in small saucepan. Let stand for 1 minute. Heat and stir on low until dissolved completely. Cool slightly.

Beat next 3 ingredients in large bowl until smooth.

Beat in gelatin mixture, white chocolate and liqueur.

Beat whipping cream in small bowl until soft peaks form. Fold into cream cheese mixture. Divide and spoon into molds. Spread evenly. Cover. Chill for at least 6 hours or overnight.

**Chocolate Sauce:** Heat first 3 ingredients in small heavy saucepan on lowest heat, stirring often, until chocolate and butter are almost melted (see page 17). Do not overheat. Remove from heat. Stir until smooth.

Stir in liqueur. Makes about 1 cup (250 mL) sauce. Invert each cheesecake onto 6 individual plates. Carefully spoon sauce around each cheesecake onto plates (see page 182).

Set 1 filigree on top of each cheesecake. Serves 6.

1 serving: 961 Calories; 73.8 g Total Fat (28.3 g Mono, 3.9 g Poly, 37.4 g Sat); 153 mg Cholesterol; 66 g Carbohydrate; 2 g Fibre; 12 g Protein; 374 mg Sodium

Pictured on page 61.

To prevent cracking as cheesecake cools, take the following precautions:

- When cheesecake is finished baking, run tip of knife between edge of cake and side of pan. This way, outer edge can settle at same rate as centre.

- Allow cheesecake to cool slowly. Let stand in pan on wire rack and let cool away from drafts, near oven (or another warm place) or place on wire rack and invert a large bowl overtop.

- If cracking does occur, cover top with whipped cream. No one will ever know!

# Chilled Desserts

Have something cool and sweet waiting in the refrigerator
while you visit with friends and family at the dinner table.
Then, bring out one of these eye-catching selections and
watch it become the centre of everyone's attention.

# Citrus Berry Zabaglione

*Vibrant red berries are covered in a foamy, pink zabaglione (zah-bahl-YOH-nay) that is made just before serving. A sweet, refreshing treat that hails from Italy.*

| | | |
|---|---|---|
| Frozen mixed berries (see Note), thawed, juice reserved | 3 cups | 750 mL |
| Sliced fresh strawberries | 1 cup | 250 mL |
| Granulated sugar | 3 tbsp. | 50 mL |
| Finely grated orange zest | 1 tsp. | 5 mL |
| Orange-flavoured liqueur (such as Grand Marnier) | 2 tbsp. | 30 mL |
| **BERRY SAUCE** | | |
| Egg yolks (large) | 5 | 5 |
| Granulated sugar | 1/4 cup | 60 mL |

Reserve 1/4 cup (60 mL) berry juice for sauce. Put mixed berries and remaining juice into medium bowl. Add next 4 ingredients. Cover. Chill for at least 6 hours or overnight, stirring occasionally.

**Berry Sauce:** Beat egg yolks and sugar in separate medium bowl over small saucepan of simmering water until well combined. Add reserved berry juice. Beat for about 5 minutes until creamy and thickened. Makes about 1 1/2 cups (375 mL) sauce. Divide berry mixture among 6 individual glasses. Divide and spoon sauce over top. Serve immediately. Serves 6.

1 serving: 182 Calories; 4.7 g Total Fat (1.7 g Mono, 0.7 g Poly, 1.3 g Sat); 180 mg Cholesterol; 31 g Carbohydrate; 4 g Fibre; 3 g Protein; 8 mg Sodium

Pictured below.

**Note:** Slice strawberries for bite-size pieces of fruit.

Bottom Left: White Chocolate Pots, page 64        Top Centre: Citrus Berry Zabaglione, above        Bottom Right: Chocolate Mousse, page 64

# White Chocolate Pots

*This smooth white chocolate mixture is totally decadent!*
*The crisp florentines are an elegant addition.*

| | | |
|---|---|---|
| Butter (or hard margarine) | 3 tbsp. | 50 mL |
| White chocolate bars (3 1/2 oz., 100 g, each), chopped | 3 | 3 |
| Egg yolks (large) | 3 | 3 |
| Orange-flavoured liqueur (such as Grand Marnier) | 2 tbsp. | 30 mL |
| Whipping cream | 1/2 cup | 125 mL |
| FLORENTINES | | |
| Sliced almonds, toasted (see Tip, page 20) | 1/4 cup | 60 mL |
| Chopped dried cranberries | 2 tbsp. | 30 mL |
| Chopped dried apricots | 2 tbsp. | 30 mL |
| Butter (or hard margarine) | 2 tbsp. | 30 mL |
| Granulated sugar | 1/3 cup | 75 mL |
| Whipping cream | 2 tsp. | 10 mL |

Heat butter and chocolate in small heavy saucepan on lowest heat, stirring often, until almost melted (see page 17). Do not overheat. Remove from heat. Stir until smooth.

Add next 3 ingredients. Stir until well combined. Divide mixture among 6 small ramekins or tea cups. Cover. Chill overnight.

**Florentines:** Combine first 3 ingredients in medium bowl.

Heat butter and sugar in separate small saucepan on medium, stirring constantly, until butter is melted and sugar is dissolved. Bring to a boil. Boil gently for about 3 minutes until mixture is starting to turn golden.

Add whipping cream. Pour over almond mixture. Mix well. Drop by heaping teaspoonfuls, about 3 inches (7.5 cm) apart, onto 2 greased cookie sheets. Bake in 350°F (175°C) oven for about 7 minutes until golden brown. Cool on cookie sheets for 1 minute. Remove to wire racks to cool. Makes about 18 cookies. Top individual servings with 1 cookie. Serve remaining cookies on the side. Serves 6.

1 serving (with 3 cookies): 556 Calories; 37.3 g Total Fat (12.3 g Mono, 1.9 g Poly, 20.5 g Sat); 171 mg Cholesterol; 49 g Carbohydrate; 1 g Fibre; 6 g Protein; 157 mg Sodium

Pictured on page 63.

# Chocolate Mousse

*This light—but rich—mousse is the perfect dessert*
*when you are too full for heavier pastries. Top with*
*whipped cream or fresh berries and shaved chocolate.*

| | | |
|---|---|---|
| Whipping cream | 1 cup | 250 mL |
| Semi-sweet chocolate baking squares (1 oz., 28 g, each), chopped | 8 | 8 |
| Butter (or hard margarine) | 1/3 cup | 75 mL |
| Egg yolks (large) | 4 | 4 |
| Vanilla | 1 tsp. | 5 mL |
| Coffee-flavoured liqueur (such as Kahlúa) | 3 tbsp. | 50 mL |
| Egg whites (large), room temperature | 4 | 4 |
| Granulated sugar | 1/3 cup | 75 mL |

Heat whipping cream in heavy medium saucepan on medium until bubbles appear around edge. Reduce to lowest heat. Add chocolate. Stir constantly until chocolate is almost melted. Do not overheat. Remove from heat. Stir until smooth.

Add butter, 1 tbsp. (15 mL) at a time, stirring constantly, until butter is melted.

Add egg yolks, 1 at a time, stirring well after each addition.

Add vanilla and liqueur. Stir. Transfer to large bowl.

Beat egg whites in separate large bowl until soft peaks form. Add sugar, 1 tbsp. (15 mL) at a time, beating well after each addition until sugar is dissolved. Fold 1/3 of egg white mixture into chocolate mixture until combined. Fold in remaining egg white mixture until no streaks remain. Divide mousse mixture among eight 3/4 cup (175 mL) ramekins. Cover. Chill for at least 6 hours or overnight. Serves 8.

1 serving: 396 Calories; 29.1 g Total Fat (9 g Mono, 1.2 g Poly, 17.1 g Sat); 166 mg Cholesterol; 31 g Carbohydrate; 2 g Fibre; 5 g Protein; 129 mg Sodium

Pictured on page 63.

# Raspberry Bavarian Cake

*The layers of white cake and pink cream are surrounded by an attractive chocolate collar. This decorative dessert is perfect for a special occasion.*

| | | |
|---|---|---|
| White cake mix (1 layer size), prepared and baked in 9 inch (22 cm) round cake pan according to package directions | 1 | 1 |
| Cherry-flavoured liqueur (such as Kirsch) or maraschino cherry syrup | 2 tbsp. | 30 mL |
| **CHOCOLATE STRIPED COLLAR (optional)** | | |
| Dark (or milk) chocolate melting wafers | 1/3 cup | 75 mL |
| Pink chocolate melting wafers | 1/3 cup | 75 mL |
| White chocolate melting wafers | 1 1/3 cups | 325 mL |
| **RASPBERRY BAVARIAN** | | |
| Envelopes of unflavoured gelatin (equivalent to 2 tbsp., 30 mL) | 2 | 2 |
| Prepared raspberry beverage | 1/3 cup | 75 mL |
| Granulated sugar | 1/2 cup | 125 mL |
| Cherry-flavoured liqueur (such as Kirsch) or maraschino cherry syrup | 2 tbsp. | 30 mL |
| Lemon juice | 2 tbsp. | 30 mL |
| Fresh (or whole frozen, thawed) raspberries | 1 lb. | 454 g |
| Whipping cream | 2 cups | 500 mL |

Cool cake. Remove from pan. Place on serving plate. Brush top of cake with liqueur.

**Chocolate Striped Collar:** Cut piece of parchment (not waxed) paper 3 3/4 × 29 inch (9.5 × 72.5 cm), marking 1 inch (2.5 cm) "tabs" at both ends. Secure to counter with tape.

Heat dark chocolate wafers in small heavy saucepan on lowest heat, stirring constantly, until almost melted. Do not overheat. Remove from heat. Stir until smooth. Pour chocolate into piping bag with ribbon tip or parchment paper cone with end snipped off. Pipe thin squiggles, about 1 inch (2.5 cm) apart, onto paper. Repeat entire process with pink chocolate wafers, piping between dark chocolate squiggles. Let stand.

Heat white chocolate wafers in clean small heavy saucepan on lowest heat, stirring constantly, until almost melted. Do not overheat. Remove from heat. Stir until smooth. Let stand for about 15 minutes, stirring occasionally, until barely warm. Pour carefully in centre down length of paper over squiggles. Carefully spread white chocolate over squiggles with offset spatula, filling spaces in between squiggles and leaving tabs uncovered. If chocolate becomes too set for shaping, use low setting on hair dryer to warm chocolate until pliable enough. Let stand for 1 to 4 minutes until slightly set, but still pliable.

Working quickly, wrap collar around cake, gently pressing ends to meet together. Do not remove paper. Chill. Pipe any remaining dark, pink and white chocolate in random squiggles on sheet of parchment paper (see page 177). Let stand at room temperature until firm.

*(continued on next page)*

**Raspberry Bavarian:** Sprinkle gelatin over raspberry beverage in separate small saucepan. Let stand for 1 minute.

Add sugar. Heat and stir on low until gelatin and sugar are dissolved completely. Remove from heat.

Stir in liqueur and lemon juice. Set aside.

Mash raspberries in large bowl. Remove some seeds, if desired, by forcing through sieve or food mill. You should have 1 1/2 cups (375 mL) raspberries and juice. Add gelatin mixture. Stir. Chill, uncovered, for about 30 minutes, stirring occasionally, until starting to thicken.

Beat whipping cream in medium bowl until soft peaks form. Fold into raspberry mixture. Makes about 6 cups (1.5 L)

bavarian. Carefully spoon onto top of cake inside chocolate collar (or make parchment paper collar). Spread evenly. Chill for at least 2 hours until set. Carefully peel parchment paper from collar. Just before serving, decorate with squiggles. Serves 12.

1 serving (without collar): 279 Calories; 15.7 g Total Fat (4.8 g Mono, 1.3 g Poly, 8.7 g Sat); 49 mg Cholesterol; 30 g Carbohydrate; 2 g Fibre; 3 g Protein; 144 mg Sodium

Pictured on this page.

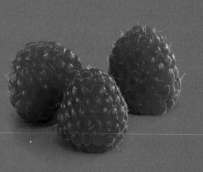

# Tiramisu

*This is an absolutely "to die for" recipe that will
leave you and your guests wanting more.
This dessert must be made ahead.*

| | | |
|---|---|---|
| Prepared strong coffee | 2 cups | 500 mL |
| Coffee-flavoured liqueur (such as Kahlúa) | 1/3 cup | 75 mL |
| Licorice-flavoured liqueur (such as Sambuca) | 1/4 cup | 60 mL |
| Package of sponge finger biscuits (such as Savoiardi) | 7 oz. | 200 g |
| Whipping cream | 1 1/2 cups | 375 mL |
| Icing (confectioner's) sugar | 1/2 cup | 125 mL |
| Mascarpone cheese | 26 oz. | 750 g |
| Coffee-flavoured liqueur (such as Kahlúa) | 2 tbsp. | 30 mL |
| Package of sponge finger biscuits (such as Savoiardi) | 7 oz. | 200 g |
| Semi-sweet chocolate baking squares (1 oz., 28 g, each), coarsely grated, chilled before and after grating | 3 | 3 |

Combine first 3 ingredients in shallow dish or medium bowl.
Dip first amount of biscuits, 1 at a time, into coffee mixture.
Reserve coffee mixture. Arrange in single layer in bottom of
ungreased 9 × 13 inch (22 × 33 cm) dish.

Beat whipping cream and icing sugar in large bowl until
soft peaks form. Add cheese and second amount of
coffee-flavoured liqueur. Mix well. Spread 1/2 of cheese
mixture over biscuits.

Dip second amount of biscuits, 1 at a time, into reserved coffee
mixture. Arrange in single layer over top of cheese mixture.
Spread with remaining cheese mixture. Cover. Chill for at least
6 hours or overnight.

Sprinkle with chocolate. Serves 12.

1 serving: 540 Calories; 37.9 g Total Fat (11.2 g Mono, 1.7 g Poly, 22.8 g Sat);
    228 mg Cholesterol; 38 g Carbohydrate; trace Fibre; 9 g Protein;
    254 mg Sodium

Pictured on page 69.

# Panna Cotta And Pears

*Pronounced PAHN-nah KOH-tah, meaning
"cooked cream" in Italian. The light, velvety custard
is accompanied by a sweet pear compote.*

### PANNA COTTA

| | | |
|---|---|---|
| Unflavoured gelatin | 2 tsp. | 10 mL |
| Milk | 1/3 cup | 75 mL |
| Milk | 2/3 cup | 150 mL |
| Whipping cream | 1 cup | 250 mL |
| Granulated sugar | 1/2 cup | 125 mL |
| Vanilla | 1 tsp. | 5 mL |

### PEAR COMPOTE

| | | |
|---|---|---|
| Port wine | 3/4 cup | 175 mL |
| Granulated sugar | 1/4 cup | 60 mL |
| Water | 1/3 cup | 75 mL |
| Peeled and chopped semi-ripe pears | 1 1/2 cups | 375 mL |
| Ground cinnamon | 1/8 tsp. | 0.5 mL |
| Ground ginger | 1/8 tsp. | 0.5 mL |

**Panna Cotta:** Lightly grease four 3/4 cup (175 mL) molds with
slightly curved or straight sides. Sprinkle gelatin over first
amount of milk in small bowl. Let stand for 1 minute.

Combine next 4 ingredients in medium saucepan. Heat and stir
on medium until sugar is dissolved and mixture is hot. Remove
from heat. Add gelatin mixture. Stir until gelatin is dissolved
completely. Strain into liquid measure. Pour into prepared
molds. Cover. Chill for at least 6 hours or overnight until set.

**Pear Compote:** Combine first 3 ingredients in medium frying
pan. Heat and stir on medium-low until sugar is dissolved.

Add remaining 3 ingredients. Boil gently on medium for about
20 minutes until thickened and pears are softened. Makes
about 1 cup (250 mL) compote. Turn into medium bowl.
Cover. Chill for at least 6 hours or overnight. To serve, unmold
Panna Cotta onto 4 individual plates. Divide and spoon
compote over custard. Serves 4.

1 serving: 481 Calories; 20.9 g Total Fat (6.1 g Mono, 0.6 g Poly, 13.1 g Sat);
    76 mg Cholesterol; 58 g Carbohydrate; 2 g Fibre; 5 g Protein; 65 mg Sodium

Pictured on page 69.

Top: Tiramisu, this page
Bottom: Panna Cotta And Pears, above

# Lemon Roll

*This elegant looking roll has a deliciously tangy lemon filling and a delicate dusting of icing sugar. Serve with fresh berries and whipped cream.*

## LEMON FILLING

| | | |
|---|---|---|
| Finely grated lemon zest | 2 tsp. | 10 mL |
| Lemon juice | 1/2 cup | 125 mL |
| Granulated sugar | 1 cup | 250 mL |
| Egg yolks (large) | 2 | 2 |
| Large eggs | 3 | 3 |
| Butter (or hard margarine), cut up | 1/2 cup | 125 mL |

## CAKE

| | | |
|---|---|---|
| Egg whites (large), room temperature | 4 | 4 |
| Granulated sugar | 1/2 cup | 125 mL |
| Egg yolks (large) | 4 | 4 |
| All-purpose flour | 1 cup | 250 mL |
| Baking powder | 2 tsp. | 10 mL |
| Warm milk | 3 tbsp. | 50 mL |
| Vanilla | 1 tsp. | 5 mL |
| Granulated sugar | 1 tbsp. | 15 mL |

Icing sugar, for dusting

**Lemon Filling:** Combine first 5 ingredients in double boiler or medium bowl. Set on saucepan of simmering water. Heat and stir for 1 to 2 minutes until warm. Do not overheat.

Add butter, 1 piece at a time, stirring constantly, until butter is melted and mixture is thickened. Cool completely. Cover. Chill for at least 8 hours or overnight. Makes about 2 cups (500 mL) filling.

**Cake:** Grease 10 x 15 inch (25 x 38 cm) jelly roll pan. Line with parchment (or waxed) paper, extending paper 2 inches (5 cm) over long sides (see page 12). Beat egg whites in medium bowl until soft peaks form. Add first amount of granulated sugar, 1 tbsp. (15 mL) at a time, beating well after each addition until sugar is dissolved.

Add egg yolks, 1 at a time, beating well after each addition until thick and light.

Add next 4 ingredients. Stir. Pour batter into prepared jelly roll pan. Spread evenly. Bake in 375°F (190°C) oven for about 10 minutes until wooden pick inserted in centre comes out clean. Let stand in pan on wire rack for 5 minutes. Run knife along sides to loosen.

Spread large tea towel on counter. Cover with sheet of parchment (or waxed) paper. Sprinkle with second amount of granulated sugar. Invert cake onto sugar. Carefully peel off and discard original parchment paper. Roll up from short end with tea towel. Let stand for about 10 minutes until cool. Unroll cake. Spread with filling to within 1 inch (2.5 cm) of each edge. Roll up from short end, using towel and paper as guide. Place, seam-side down, on long 12 inch (30 cm) serving plate or cake board (see page 184).

Dust with icing sugar. Cut, with serrated knife, into generous 1 inch (2.5 cm) thick slices. Serves 8.

1 serving: 416 Calories; 18.1 g Total Fat (5.7 g Mono, 1.3 g Poly, 9.4 g Sat); 275 mg Cholesterol; 56 g Carbohydrate; 1 g Fibre; 8 g Protein; 277 mg Sodium

Pictured on page 71.

# Coconut Soufflé Mousse

*This molded mousse is textured with bits of coconut. For a special presentation, serve on a bed of Raspberry Sauce, page 128, or fill centre of unmolded mousse with fresh berries. This may also be frozen for a delicious coconut ice cream.*

| | | |
|---|---|---|
| Unflavoured gelatin | 4 tsp. | 20 mL |
| Malibu rum (or other coconut-flavoured rum) | 1/4 cup | 60 mL |
| Unsweetened coconut cream (available in Asian section of grocery store) | 2 cups | 500 mL |
| Fine unsweetened coconut | 1/2 cup | 125 mL |
| Granulated sugar | 1/4 cup | 60 mL |
| Egg yolks (large) | 3 | 3 |
| Butter (or hard margarine) | 1 tbsp. | 15 mL |
| Coconut flavouring (or vanilla) | 1 tsp. | 5 mL |
| Egg whites (large), room temperature | 3 | 3 |
| Granulated sugar | 1/3 cup | 75 mL |
| Whipping cream | 1 cup | 250 mL |

Lightly grease 6 cup (1.5 L) mold. Sprinkle gelatin over rum in small saucepan. Let stand for 1 minute. Heat and stir on low until dissolved completely. Cool slightly.

Combine next 4 ingredients in medium saucepan. Heat on medium, stirring occasionally, until just starting to boil and thicken. Remove from heat.

Add butter and flavouring. Stir until butter is melted. Stir in gelatin mixture. Transfer to large bowl. Cover with plastic wrap directly on surface to prevent skin from forming. Cool for about 1 hour until room temperature.

Beat egg whites in medium bowl until soft peaks form. Add second amount of sugar, 1 tbsp. (15 mL) at a time, beating well after each addition until sugar is dissolved. Fold 1/3 of egg white mixture into coconut mixture. Fold in remaining egg white mixture.

Beat whipping cream with same beaters in same medium bowl until stiff peaks form. Fold into coconut mixture. Turn into greased 6 cup (1.5 L) mold. Chill for at least 8 hours or overnight until set. To unmold, dip in very warm water for about 15 seconds. Invert onto plate. Chill until ready to serve. Serves 10.

1 serving: 373 Calories; 31.5 g Total Fat (4.2 g Mono, 0.7 g Poly, 24.6 g Sat); 97 mg Cholesterol; 20 g Carbohydrate; 1 g Fibre; 6 g Protein; 47 mg Sodium

Pictured below.

Top: Coconut Soufflé Mousse, page 70
Bottom: Lemon Roll, page 70

# Layered Chocolate Terrine

*Two layers of chocolate decadence—dark and white—are encased in a crunchy praline. Indulge in this rich dessert and you'll be glad you did!*

### BOTTOM LAYER

| | | |
|---|---|---|
| Whipping cream | 1/3 cup | 75 mL |
| Almond-flavoured liqueur (such as Amaretto) | 2 tbsp. | 30 mL |
| Milk chocolate bars (3 1/2 oz., 100 g, each), chopped | 3 | 3 |

### TOP LAYER

| | | |
|---|---|---|
| Whipping cream | 1/3 cup | 75 mL |
| Almond-flavoured liqueur (such as Amaretto) | 2 tbsp. | 30 mL |
| White chocolate bars (3 1/2 oz., 100 g, each), chopped | 3 | 3 |

### MIXED NUT PRALINE

| | | |
|---|---|---|
| Macadamia nuts, toasted (see Tip, page 20) and chopped | 1/3 cup | 75 mL |
| Slivered almonds, toasted (see Tip, page 20) | 1/3 cup | 75 mL |
| Granulated sugar | 2/3 cup | 150 mL |
| Water | 1/3 cup | 75 mL |

### CARAMEL CUSTARD SAUCE

| | | |
|---|---|---|
| Half-and-half cream | 3/4 cup | 175 mL |
| Egg yolks (large) | 3 | 3 |
| Dark brown (not golden) sugar, packed | 3 tbsp. | 50 mL |

**Bottom Layer:** Line 7 x 3 x 2 inch (18 x 7.5 x 5 cm) foil loaf pan with plastic wrap, leaving several inches hanging over all sides. Heat whipping cream in medium saucepan on medium-low until very hot and bubbles appear around edge. Remove from heat. Add liqueur and milk chocolate. Stir until smooth. Cool for about 1 1/4 hours until mixture will hold its shape. Spoon into prepared pan. Spread evenly. Set aside.

**Top Layer:** Heat whipping cream in separate medium saucepan on medium-low until very hot and bubbles appear around edge. Remove from heat. Add liqueur and white chocolate. Stir until smooth. Cool for about 1 1/4 hours until mixture will hold its shape. Spoon over milk chocolate layer. Carefully spread evenly. Chill for about 1 1/2 hours until set.

**Mixed Nut Praline** (see how-to photo, page 16): Spread macadamia nuts and almonds, touching, on lightly greased baking sheet.

Heat sugar and water in heavy medium saucepan on medium-low, stirring constantly, until sugar is dissolved. Bring to a boil on medium-high. Boil, uncovered, for 5 to 10 minutes, without stirring, until deep golden brown. Drizzle over nuts. Let stand for 20 minutes until hard. Break into pieces. Process in food processor until finely chopped or put into plastic bag and crush with mallet or rolling pin. Makes about 1 cup (250 mL) praline. Spread praline on large sheet of waxed paper. Using plastic wrap to lift out terrine, invert onto praline. Use edges of waxed paper to flip terrine around until all sides are coated with praline. Using waxed paper, carefully lift onto serving plate. Chill for at least 8 hours until set. Let stand on counter for about 1 1/2 hours before cutting.

**Caramel Custard Sauce:** Heat cream in small saucepan on medium, stirring occasionally, until very hot and bubbles appear around edge.

Combine egg yolks and brown sugar in small bowl. Gradually add hot cream, whisking until mixed. Return to saucepan. Heat and stir on low for 2 to 3 minutes until starting to thicken. Remove from heat. Cool, uncovered, for 10 minutes. Strain sauce into separate small bowl. Cover with plastic wrap directly on surface to prevent skin from forming. Chill until cold. Makes 3/4 cup (175 mL) sauce. Drizzle about 1 tbsp. (15 mL) on each of 12 individual plates. Cut terrine into twelve 1/2 inch (12 mm) slices. Cut each slice in half diagonally. Set triangles on sauce. Serves 12.

1 serving: 444 Calories; 27.5 g Total Fat (10.7 g Mono, 1.3 g Poly, 13.9 g Sat); 86 mg Cholesterol; 44 g Carbohydrate; 1 g Fibre; 6 g Protein; 58 mg Sodium

Pictured on page 73.

*Chilled Desserts*

# Poached Pear Delight

*This is a mellow, aromatic dessert with a delicious ginger ice cream.*

| | | |
|---|---|---|
| Vanilla bean, split in half lengthwise (or 1/2 tsp., 2 mL, vanilla) | 1 | 1 |
| Sweet dessert white wine (such as late harvest dessert wine) | 2 cups | 500 mL |
| Brown sugar, packed | 3 tbsp. | 50 mL |
| Cinnamon stick (4 inch, 10 cm, length) | 1 | 1 |
| Firm medium pears, peeled (leave stems attached) | 4 | 4 |
| **GINGER ICE CREAM** | | |
| Sliced almonds | 1/3 cup | 75 mL |
| Maple (or maple-flavoured) syrup | 1 1/2 tbsp. | 25 mL |
| Ground cinnamon | 1/4 tsp. | 1 mL |
| Vanilla ice cream, softened | 2 cups | 500 mL |
| Finely chopped crystallized ginger | 3 tbsp. | 50 mL |

Combine first 4 ingredients in medium saucepan. Heat and stir on medium-high until brown sugar is dissolved.

Add pears. Bring to a boil. Reduce heat to medium-low. Cover. Cook for about 30 minutes, turning several times, until pears are tender. Remove pears from poaching liquid to heatproof medium bowl. Remove and discard cinnamon stick and vanilla bean. Boil poaching liquid on high for about 10 minutes, without stirring, until slightly thickened. Pour over pears. Cool. Cover. Chill for at least 8 hours or overnight, turning pears occasionally.

**Ginger Ice Cream:** Line baking sheet with parchment (or waxed) paper. Combine first 3 ingredients in small bowl. Place on prepared baking sheet. Cook in 375°F (190°C) oven for about 10 minutes, stirring once, until almonds are golden. Cool. Chop.

Put ice cream, ginger and almond mixture into separate medium bowl. Mix well. Cover. Freeze for 8 hours or overnight until firm. About 30 minutes before serving, remove pears and liquid from refrigerator. Just before serving, divide pears among 4 individual bowls. Divide and drizzle poaching liquid over pears. Add 2 scoops of ice cream to each bowl beside pears. Serves 4.

1 serving: 513 Calories; 12.6 g Total Fat (5.4 g Mono, 1.3 g Poly, 5.2 g Sat); 31 mg Cholesterol; 65 g Carbohydrate; 4 g Fibre; 5 g Protein; 79 mg Sodium

Pictured on this page.

Top: Poached Pear Delight, this page
Bottom: Layered Chocolate Terrine, page 72

*Chilled Desserts*

# Mocha Bavarian Dessert

*A creamy coffee-coloured mousse is layered over a white speckled cake. The flavours of almond, chocolate and coffee blend perfectly.*

### SPONGE CAKE

| | | |
|---|---|---|
| Large eggs | 2 | 2 |
| Granulated sugar | 1 cup | 250 mL |
| All-purpose flour | 1 cup | 250 mL |
| Baking powder | 1 tsp. | 5 mL |
| Milk | 1/2 cup | 125 mL |
| Butter (or hard margarine) | 1 tbsp. | 15 mL |
| Bittersweet chocolate baking square, finely grated (chilled before and after grating) | 1 oz. | 28 g |

### MOCHA NUT BAVARIAN

| | | |
|---|---|---|
| Homogenized milk | 1 1/2 cups | 375 mL |
| Instant coffee granules | 2 tsp. | 10 mL |
| Granulated sugar | 1/2 cup | 125 mL |
| Cocoa, sifted if lumpy | 2 tbsp. | 30 mL |
| Salt, sprinkle | | |
| Egg yolks (large) | 2 | 2 |
| Envelopes of unflavoured gelatin (equivalent to 2 tbsp., 30 mL) | 2 | 2 |
| Homogenized milk | 1/2 cup | 125 mL |
| Vanilla | 1/2 tsp. | 2 mL |
| Sliced almonds, toasted (see Tip, page 20) | 1/4 cup | 60 mL |
| Egg whites (large), room temperature | 2 | 2 |
| Salt | 1/8 tsp. | 0.5 mL |
| Granulated sugar | 1/4 cup | 60 mL |
| Whipping cream | 1 cup | 250 mL |
| Cocoa, for garnish | | |

**Sponge Cake:** Grease 9 inch (22 cm) round cake pan. Line bottom with parchment (not waxed) paper (see page 12). Beat eggs in medium bowl on high for about 5 minutes until increased in volume. Add sugar while beating, 1 tbsp. (15 mL) at a time, until pale and thickened.

Add flour and baking powder. Beat on low until mixed.

Heat milk and butter in small saucepan until very hot and bubbles appear around edge. Slowly add to flour mixture while beating on low. Beat for about 1 minute until mixed.

Fold chocolate into batter. Spread evenly in prepared pan. Bake in 350°F (175°C) oven for 25 to 30 minutes until wooden pick inserted in centre comes out clean. Let stand in pan on wire rack until cool. Invert cake onto rack. Peel off and discard paper. Place cake upright on serving plate. Fold 30 inch (75 cm) length of parchment (or waxed) paper lengthwise into thirds until about 4 inches (10 cm) wide. Secure around cake with string, forming "collar" above cake to contain filling.

**Mocha Nut Bavarian:** Heat first amount of milk and instant coffee in medium saucepan on medium, stirring occasionally, until hot.

Combine next 4 ingredients in small bowl. Add about 1/2 cup (125 mL) hot milk mixture. Mix well. Whisk into milk mixture. Heat and stir until just boiling. Remove from heat.

Sprinkle gelatin over second amount of milk in separate small bowl. Stir. Let stand for 1 minute. Stir.

Add gelatin mixture and vanilla to hot milk mixture. Stir until gelatin is dissolved completely. Turn into separate medium bowl. Chill, uncovered, for about 1 hour, stirring occasionally, until syrupy and starting to thicken.

Fold in almonds.

Beat egg whites and second amount of salt in large bowl until foamy. Add second amount of sugar, 1 tbsp. (15 mL) at a time, beating well after each addition until soft peaks form. Fold cooled chocolate mixture into egg white mixture.

Beat whipping cream in separate small bowl with same beaters until stiff peaks form. Fold into chocolate mixture. Pour over cake inside collar. Smooth top. Chill for at least 8 hours or overnight until set.

Just before serving, remove collar. Sprinkle 10 individual plates with cocoa (see page 183). Cut dessert into 10 wedges with hot knife. Set individual wedges on cocoa. Serves 10.

1 serving: 383 Calories; 15.7 g Total Fat (5.3 g Mono, 1 g Poly, 8.3 g Sat); 126 mg Cholesterol; 54 g Carbohydrate; 1 g Fibre; 9 g Protein; 150 mg Sodium

Pictured on page 75.

# Margarita Parfaits

*Serve these tart parfaits in classy margarita glasses. This "adults only" dessert will be a hit at your next dinner party.*

## LIME CREAM

| | | |
|---|---|---|
| Granulated sugar | 1/3 cup | 75 mL |
| Cornstarch | 1 tsp. | 5 mL |
| Lime juice | 2 tbsp. | 30 mL |
| Finely grated lime zest | 1 1/2 tsp. | 7 mL |
| Tequila | 1 tbsp. | 15 mL |
| Orange-flavoured liqueur (such as Grand Marnier) | 1 tbsp. | 15 mL |
| Egg yolks (large) | 2 | 2 |
| Whipping cream | 1 cup | 250 mL |

## STRAWBERRY CREAM

| | | |
|---|---|---|
| Granulated sugar | 1/3 cup | 75 mL |
| Cornstarch | 2 tsp. | 10 mL |
| Fresh whole (or frozen, thawed) strawberries, puréed in blender | 10 | 10 |
| Tequila | 1 tbsp. | 15 mL |
| Orange-flavoured liqueur (such as Grand Marnier) | 1 tbsp. | 15 mL |
| Egg yolks (large) | 2 | 2 |
| Drops of red food colouring (optional) | 2 | 2 |

## GARNISH

| | | |
|---|---|---|
| Coloured sanding (decorating) sugar (see Note) | 1/4 cup | 60 mL |
| Lime wedge | 1 | 1 |
| Lime zest twists | 4 | 4 |
| Fresh whole strawberries | 4 | 4 |

**Lime Cream:** Combine sugar and cornstarch in small saucepan. Whisk in next 5 ingredients. Heat on medium for 3 to 4 minutes, stirring constantly, until thickened and just starting to boil. Remove from heat. Transfer to small bowl. Cover with plastic wrap directly on surface to prevent skin from forming. Chill for about 1 1/2 hours until cold.

Beat whipping cream in medium bowl until stiff peaks form. Fold 1/2 of whipped cream into lime mixture. Reserve remaining whipped cream for Strawberry Cream, below. Makes 2 cups (500 mL) Lime Cream.

**Strawberry Cream:** Combine sugar and cornstarch in separate small saucepan. Add strawberry purée. Stir well.

Whisk in tequila, liqueur and egg yolks. Heat on medium for 3 to 4 minutes, stirring constantly, until thickened and just starting to boil. Remove from heat. Transfer to separate small bowl.

Stir in food colouring. Cover with plastic wrap directly on surface to prevent skin from forming. Chill for about 1 1/2 hours until cold. Fold in reserved whipped cream. Makes 2 cups (500 mL) Strawberry Cream.

**Garnish:** Measure sanding sugar into shallow dish. Rub lime wedge around rims of 4 margarita glasses. Dip each glass rim into sanding sugar. Spoon generous 1/3 cup (75 mL) each of Lime Cream and Strawberry Cream, side by side, into glass.

Drag wooden pick or skewer from centre of one colour to centre of other colour. Repeat dragging in opposite directions until feather look is achieved.

Garnish each with lime zest twist and strawberry. Serves 4.

1 serving: 455 Calories; 25.5 g Total Fat (7.9 g Mono, 1.4 g Poly, 14.2 g Sat); 289 mg Cholesterol; 46 g Carbohydrate; 1 g Fibre; 4 g Protein; 31 mg Sodium

**Note:** Sanding sugar is a coarse decorating sugar that resembles the coloured sugar frequently used at Christmastime. It gives a special look to fancy desserts and pastries. Available in specialty kitchen stores.

Pictured on page 77.

# Peach Coconut Trifles

*A fantastic looking dish with a tempting mix of refreshing flavours. Layers of custard are alternated with peaches and cookie crumbs. A heavy dessert that can serve 8 if desired.*

### COCONUT CUSTARD

| | | |
|---|---|---|
| Egg yolks (large) | 4 | 4 |
| Granulated sugar | 1/3 cup | 75 mL |
| Can of coconut milk | 14 oz. | 398 mL |
| Coconut cookies, broken up (makes about 2 cups, 500 mL) | 18 | 18 |
| Cans of sliced peaches (14 oz., 398 mL, each), drained | 2 | 2 |

Coconut Curls (page 180), toasted
(see Tip, page 20)

**Coconut Custard:** Beat egg yolks and sugar in medium bowl until thick and creamy.

Bring coconut milk to a boil in medium saucepan. Gradually whisk into egg yolk mixture. Return to same saucepan. Heat and stir on medium, being careful not to boil, until thickened and coats back of spoon. Turn into separate medium bowl. Cover. Chill for about 3 hours until cold. Makes about 1 3/4 cups (425 mL) custard.

Divide 1/2 of broken cookies among 4 individual glasses. Spoon about 2 tbsp. (30 mL) custard over cookies in each glass. Add 2 peach slices to each. Repeat layers, finishing with peach slices. Cover. Chill for at least 6 hours or overnight.

Garnish with coconut curls. Serves 4.

1 serving: 800 Calories; 39.2 g Total Fat (3.5 g Mono, 1.1 g Poly, 31.7 g Sat); 216 mg Cholesterol; 111 g Carbohydrate; 2 g Fibre; 9 g Protein; 293 mg Sodium

Pictured on this page.

Top: Margarita Parfaits, page 76
Bottom: Peach Coconut Trifles, above

# Strawberry Flowers

*This delicate dessert is elegantly presented.*
*Dainty chocolate leaves surround fresh strawberries*
*filled with a silky almond custard.*

## ALMOND CUSTARD FILLING

| | | |
|---|---|---|
| Cornstarch | 1 tbsp. | 15 mL |
| All-purpose flour | 1 tbsp. | 15 mL |
| Granulated sugar | 1/4 cup | 60 mL |
| Salt | 1/16 tsp. | 0.5 mL |
| Homogenized milk | 3/4 cup | 175 mL |
| Egg yolk (large) | 1 | 1 |
| Butter (or hard margarine) | 1 tsp. | 5 mL |
| Almond flavouring | 1/2 tsp. | 2 mL |
| Fresh whole large strawberries | 12 | 12 |

## CHOCOLATE FILIGREES

| | | |
|---|---|---|
| Dark chocolate melting wafers (or semi-sweet chocolate chips) | 3/4 cup | 175 mL |

**Almond Custard Filling:** Combine first 4 ingredients in small saucepan. Gradually stir in milk. Heat on medium for about 5 minutes, stirring constantly, until boiling and thickened. Remove from heat.

Beat egg yolk with fork in small cup. Add large spoonful of hot milk mixture to egg yolk. Mix well. Stir into milk mixture. Heat and stir on medium-low for 1 minute until thickened. Remove from heat.

Stir in butter and flavouring. Cover with plastic wrap directly on surface to prevent skin from forming. Makes 3/4 cup (175 mL) filling.

Slice hulls from strawberries, making flat base for strawberries to stand upright. Make 3 crosscuts (✻) from tip of each berry almost, but not quite through, to base. Carefully spread cuts open to make 6 "petals." Pipe about 1 tbsp. (15 mL) filling into centre of each berry. Cover. Chill.

**Chocolate Filigrees:** Heat chocolate in small heavy saucepan on lowest heat, stirring often, until almost melted (see page 177). Do not overheat. Remove from heat. Stir until smooth.

Using parchment paper cone (see page 176) or small resealable freezer bag with small snipped corner, pipe about 1/4 of melted chocolate into 9 medium-sized petal outlines on narrow strip of waxed paper (see page 177). Immediately lay over rolling pin or other curved object. If filigrees will not fall into curve, warm with hair dryer. Chill for 10 minutes before carefully removing from rolling pin. Peel off paper. Transfer filigrees to plates. Repeat 3 more times to make a total of 36 petals, rewarming chocolate on low as necessary.

Arrange 9 petals on each of 4 individual plates to hold 3 strawberries each. Use small dab of warmed leftover chocolate to anchor petals and strawberries onto plates. Chill for up to 2 hours until ready to serve. Serves 4.

1 serving: 298 Calories; 14.1 g Total Fat (4.6 g Mono, 0.7 g Poly, 7.9 g Sat); 63 mg Cholesterol; 44 g Carbohydrate; 3 g Fibre; 4 g Protein; 79 mg Sodium

Pictured on page 79.

**Variation:** Instead of making individual filigree petals, squeeze chocolate designs directly onto individual plates and anchor strawberries with small dab of melted chocolate.

# Pistachio Dessert

*A colourful, summery dessert that is very light and fresh.*

## PISTACHIO CAKE

| | | |
|---|---|---|
| White cake mix (1 layer size) | 1 | 1 |
| Instant pistachio pudding powder (4 serving size) | 1 | 1 |
| Water | 1/2 cup | 125 mL |
| Cooking oil | 1/4 cup | 60 mL |
| Large eggs | 2 | 2 |

## MOUSSE LAYER

| | | |
|---|---|---|
| Envelope of unflavoured gelatin (equivalent to 1 tbsp., 15 mL) | 1 | 1 |
| Lemon juice | 1/4 cup | 60 mL |
| Water | 2/3 cup | 150 mL |
| Water | 1/3 cup | 75 mL |
| Granulated sugar | 2/3 cup | 150 mL |
| Finely grated lemon zest | 4 1/2 tsp. | 22 mL |
| Egg yolks (large) | 2 | 2 |
| Egg whites (large), room temperature | 2 | 2 |
| Whipped cream (or frozen whipped topping, thawed) | 2 cups | 500 mL |
| Chopped pistachios, for garnish | 1/2 cup | 125 mL |

**Pistachio Cake:** Grease 9 inch (22 cm) springform pan. Set pan on piece of foil, bringing up foil and pressing firmly against outside of pan to prevent leaking. Put all 5 ingredients into medium bowl. Beat until smooth. Pour evenly into prepared pan. Bake in 350°F (175°C) oven for about 30 minutes until wooden pick inserted in centre comes out clean. Let stand in pan on wire rack until cool. Do not remove from pan.

**Mousse Layer:** Sprinkle gelatin over lemon juice and first amount of water in medium saucepan. Let stand for 1 minute. Heat and stir on medium until gelatin is dissolved completely.

Mix next 4 ingredients in small bowl. Stir into gelatin mixture. Heat and stir until boiling and slightly thickened. Cool in saucepan until syrupy.

Beat egg whites in separate small bowl until stiff (not dry) peaks form. Fold into egg yolk mixture. Fold in whipped cream. Spread evenly over cake.

Sprinkle pistachios over mousse. Chill for at least 6 hours or overnight. Remove to serving plate. Cuts into 12 wedges.

1 wedge: 306 Calories; 18.6 g Total Fat (8.4 g Mono, 3.1 g Poly, 6 g Sat); 97 mg Cholesterol; 31 g Carbohydrate; trace Fibre; 5 g Protein; 171 mg Sodium

Pictured on page 81.

# Cherry Cheese Dessert

*An old-fashioned dessert, reminiscent of jam scones and clotted cream. The layers of red and white are very pretty!*

## CAKE LAYER

| | | |
|---|---|---|
| All-purpose flour | 1/2 cup | 125 mL |
| Granulated sugar | 1/2 cup | 125 mL |
| Baking powder | 1/2 tsp. | 2 mL |
| Salt | 1/4 tsp. | 1 mL |
| Milk | 1/4 cup | 60 mL |
| Cooking oil | 2 tsp. | 10 mL |
| Large egg | 1 | 1 |
| Vanilla | 1/2 tsp. | 2 mL |

## CHEESE LAYER

| | | |
|---|---|---|
| Block of cream cheese | 8 oz. | 250 g |
| Icing (confectioner's) sugar | 1 cup | 250 mL |
| Vanilla | 1/2 tsp. | 2 mL |
| Whipping cream (or 2 cups, 250 mL, frozen whipped topping, thawed) | 1 cup | 250 mL |

## TOPPING

| | | |
|---|---|---|
| Whipping cream (or 1 cup, 250 mL, frozen whipped topping, thawed) | 1/2 cup | 125 mL |
| Can of cherry pie filling | 19 oz. | 540 mL |

**Cake Layer:** Grease 9 inch (22 cm) springform pan. Set pan on piece of foil, bringing up foil and pressing firmly against outside of pan to prevent leaking. Measure all 8 ingredients into medium bowl. Beat until smooth. Pour into prepared pan. Bake in 350°F (175°C) oven for about 30 minutes until lightly golden and wooden pick inserted in centre comes out clean. Let stand in pan on wire rack until cool. Do not remove from pan.

**Cheese Layer:** Beat cream cheese, icing sugar and vanilla in separate medium bowl for about 5 minutes until fluffy.

Beat whipping cream in small bowl until stiff peaks form. Fold into cream cheese mixture. Spread over cooled cake.

**Topping:** Beat whipping cream in separate small bowl until stiff peaks form. Spoon into piping bag fitted with closed star tip. Pipe rosettes around outer edge of cake (see page 175).

Strain cherry pie filling through sieve until about 1 cup (250 mL) cherries remain. Discard cherry sauce. Arrange cherries inside of rosettes in even layer. Chill for at least 1 hour before serving. Remove to serving plate. Cuts into 12 wedges.

1 wedge: 258 Calories; 13.7 g Total Fat (4.2 g Mono, 0.7 g Poly, 8 g Sat); 59 mg Cholesterol; 32 g Carbohydrate; trace Fibre; 3 g Protein; 142 mg Sodium

Pictured on page 81.

Top: Cherry Cheese Dessert, above
Bottom: Pistachio Dessert, this page

# Creamy Desserts

Velvety smooth and popular with all ages,
these desserts bring a creamy touch to any dinner menu.
Show them off in stylish glasses, plates or bowls and give them
some artistic flair by adding a few attractive garnishes.

# Mascarpone Fruit Dip

*Dip fresh, seasonal fruit into the smooth,
creamy cheese mixture and then into the sweet praline.
This is a fun, easy-to-make dessert.*

### MASCARPONE DIP

| | | |
|---|---|---|
| Tub of mascarpone cheese, softened | 1 lb. | 500 g |
| Whipping cream | 1/2 cup | 125 mL |
| Orange-flavoured liqueur (such as Grand Marnier) | 2 tbsp. | 30 mL |
| Icing (confectioner's) sugar | 1/4 cup | 60 mL |

### ALMOND PECAN PRALINE

| | | |
|---|---|---|
| Whole blanched almonds, toasted (see Tip, page 20) | 1/2 cup | 125 mL |
| Pecan halves, toasted (see Tip, page 20) | 1/2 cup | 125 mL |
| Granulated sugar | 1 cup | 250 mL |
| Water | 1/3 cup | 75 mL |

**Cut fresh fruit (your choice), for dipping**

**Mascarpone Dip:** Combine all 4 ingredients in medium bowl. Makes about 2 1/2 cups (625 mL) dip.

**Almond Pecan Praline** (see how-to photos, page 16)**:** Spread almonds and pecan halves in single layer, touching, on lightly greased baking sheet.

Heat granulated sugar and water in medium saucepan on medium-low, stirring constantly, until sugar is dissolved. Boil on medium-high for 5 to 10 minutes, without stirring, until deep golden brown. Pour evenly over nuts. Let stand for 20 minutes until hard. Break into pieces. Process in food processor until coarse crumbs or put into plastic bag and crush with mallet or rolling pin. Makes about 2 cups (500 mL) praline.

Arrange fruit on platter. Put dip and praline into separate small serving bowls. Serves 12.

1 serving (dip only): 193 Calories; 17.9 g Total Fat (5.1 g Mono, 0.6 g Poly, 11.3 g Sat); 58 mg Cholesterol; 4 g Carbohydrate; 0 g Fibre; 3 g Protein; 127 mg Sodium

1 serving (praline only): 137 Calories; 6.6 g Total Fat (4.2 g Mono, 1.5 g Poly, 0.6 g Sat); 0 mg Cholesterol; 20 g Carbohydrate; 1 g Fibre; 2 g Protein; 1 mg Sodium

Pictured on this page

# Peach Pistachio Cornets

*Crisp wafer cones are edged in white chocolate and dipped into pistachios for a very attractive look. The soft filling is similar to cheesecake in texture and flavour.*

### TUILE CORNETS

| | | |
|---|---|---|
| Egg whites (large), room temperature | 2 | 2 |
| Granulated sugar | 6 tbsp. | 100 mL |
| Salt, just a pinch | | |
| Almond flavouring | 1/4 tsp. | 1 mL |
| Butter (or hard margarine), melted | 1/4 cup | 60 mL |
| All-purpose flour | 1/2 cup | 125 mL |
| Finely chopped pistachios | 2/3 cup | 150 mL |
| White chocolate melting wafers | 1 cup | 250 mL |

### PEACH FILLING

| | | |
|---|---|---|
| Can of peaches in syrup | 14 oz. | 398 mL |
| Envelope of unflavoured gelatin (equivalent to 1 tbsp., 15 mL) | 1 | 1 |
| Icing (confectioner's) sugar | 1/4 cup | 60 mL |
| Peach schnapps liqueur (or peach nectar) | 2 tbsp. | 30 mL |
| Whipping cream | 1/2 cup | 125 mL |
| Block of cream cheese, softened | 4 oz. | 125 g |

**Tuile Cornets** (see pages 178 and 179): Cut 2 circles, 4 1/4 inches (10.6 cm) in diameter, from heavier paper. Shape each into cone. Tape securely. Line bottom of baking sheet with parchment (not waxed) paper. Trace two 4 1/4 inch (10.6 cm) circles, about 3 inches (7.5 cm) apart, on paper. Turn paper over. Whisk first 4 ingredients in medium bowl until frothy.

Whisk in butter. Add flour. Whisk until smooth. Drop 1 tbsp. (15 mL) batter onto each circle. Spread evenly with offset spatula (see page 11) to fill circles.

Sprinkle each circle with 1/2 tsp. (2 mL) pistachios. Bake in 350°F (175°C) oven for 7 to 8 minutes until lightly browned. Place folded tea towel on counter. Working quickly, slide offset spatula under 1 circle. Lift and place on towel. Immediately place paper cone on circle. Roll around cone, using tea towel as guide (see page 179). Repeat with second circle. Let stand for about 2 minutes until cooled and crisp. Remove paper cones to reuse. Repeat entire process with remaining batter, for a total of 16 cornets. Reserve remaining pistachios for dipping.

Heat white chocolate wafers in small heavy saucepan on lowest heat, stirring often, until almost melted. Do not overheat. Remove from heat. Stir until smooth. Pour chocolate into shallow dish. Put reserved pistachios into separate shallow dish. Dip about 1/4 inch (6 mm) of rounded edge of each cone into chocolate. Immediately dip chocolate edge into pistachios while still wet. Place on waxed paper to dry. If chocolate becomes too cool, heat in microwave on medium (50%) for a few seconds, stirring often, until warm. Makes 16 cornets.

**Peach Filling:** Drain peaches, reserving 1/2 cup (125 mL) syrup in small saucepan. Discard remaining syrup or reserve for another use. Sprinkle gelatin over syrup in saucepan. Let stand for 1 minute. Add icing sugar. Heat and stir on medium until gelatin is completely dissolved. Remove from heat.

Add liqueur. Stir. Process peaches and gelatin mixture in blender until smooth. Transfer to small bowl. Chill for about 45 minutes, stirring occasionally, until starting to thicken.

Beat whipping cream in separate small bowl until soft peaks form.

Beat cream cheese in medium bowl until smooth. Add whipped cream. Beat on low until combined. Beat in peach mixture. Makes 3 cups (750 mL) filling. Chill for at least 1 hour. Pipe filling into cornets (see page 15). Cornets may be filled and chilled for up to 2 hours before serving. Makes 16 filled cornets.

1 filled cornet: 232 Calories; 14.7 g Total Fat (5.5 g Mono, 0.9 g Poly, 7.5 g Sat); 28 mg Cholesterol; 22 g Carbohydrate; 1 g Fibre; 4 g Protein; 75 mg Sodium

Pictured on page 85.

# Crème Brûlée

*Pronounced krehm broo-LAY, these words literally mean "burnt cream." The sugary topping is broiled to create a wonderful, brittle contrast to the creamy custard underneath.*

| | | |
|---|---|---|
| Egg yolks (large) | 6 | 6 |
| Granulated sugar | 1/3 cup | 75 mL |
| Whipping cream | 1 cup | 250 mL |
| Half-and-half cream | 1 cup | 250 mL |
| Vanilla | 1/2 tsp. | 2 mL |
| Granulated sugar | 1/4 cup | 60 mL |

Grease six 3/4 cup (175 mL) ovenproof ramekins. Place in ovenproof pan large enough to hold ramekins. Whisk egg yolks and first amount of sugar in large bowl until sugar is dissolved and mixture is frothy.

Add next 3 ingredients. Whisk until well combined. Divide among ramekins. Carefully pour enough boiling water into pan

until water comes halfway up sides of ramekins. Bake in 325°F (160°C) oven for about 40 minutes until almost set. Filling may still wobble in middle, but will set upon cooling. Remove from water. Cool completely. Cover. Chill for at least 6 hours or overnight.

Divide and sprinkle second amount of sugar over top. Broil on top rack in oven for about 3 minutes until sugar is browned and bubbling. Let stand for 5 minutes before serving. Serves 6.

1 serving: 317 Calories; 22.9 g Total Fat (7.1 g Mono, 1.3 g Poly, 12.7 g Sat); 278 mg Cholesterol; 24 g Carbohydrate; 0 g Fibre; 5 g Protein; 40 mg Sodium

Pictured on page 87.

# White Chocolate Crème Brûlée

*This rich, pale custard is topped with a caramelized, golden crust. The textures are delicate and delicious!*

| | | |
|---|---|---|
| Whipping cream | 2 cups | 500 mL |
| White chocolate baking squares (1 oz., 28 g, each), chopped | 6 | 6 |
| Granulated sugar | 1/4 cup | 60 mL |
| Egg yolks (large), fork-beaten | 6 | 6 |
| Vanilla | 1 tsp. | 5 mL |
| Granulated sugar | 3 tbsp. | 50 mL |

Grease six 1/2 cup (125 mL) ovenproof ramekins. Place in ovenproof pan large enough to hold ramekins. Heat whipping cream in medium saucepan on medium until very hot and bubbles appear around edge. Remove from heat. Add chocolate and first amount of sugar. Stir until chocolate is melted.

Add egg yolk and vanilla. Whisk until well combined. Divide custard among ramekins. Carefully pour enough boiling water into pan until water comes halfway up sides of ramekins. Bake in 300°F (150°C) oven for 40 to 45 minutes until almost set. Filling may still wobble in middle, but will set upon cooling. Remove from water. Cool completely. Cover. Chill for at least 6 hours or overnight.

Divide and sprinkle second amount of sugar over top. Broil on top rack in oven for about 3 minutes until sugar is browned and bubbling. Let stand for 5 minutes. Serves 6.

1 serving: 571 Calories; 47.9 g Total Fat (14.6 g Mono, 2 g Poly, 28.1 g Sat); 354 mg Cholesterol; 31 g Carbohydrate; 0 g Fibre; 6 g Protein; 66 mg Sodium

Pictured on page 87.

Top: Crème Brûlée, this page
Bottom: White Chocolate Crème Brûlée, above

# Rhubarb And Cinnamon Custards

*The warm cinnamon flavour of the sweet custards goes well with the tartness of the compote. The custards may be made the day before and kept chilled until ready to serve.*

| | | |
|---|---|---|
| Unflavoured gelatin | 1 1/2 tsp. | 7 mL |
| Half-and-half cream | 1/4 cup | 60 mL |
| | | |
| Half-and-half cream | 1 3/4 cups | 425 mL |
| Granulated sugar | 1/2 cup | 125 mL |
| | | |
| Ground cinnamon, sprinkle | | |

**RHUBARB COMPOTE**

| | | |
|---|---|---|
| Frozen rhubarb, thawed and drained | 6 tbsp. | 100 mL |
| Dried cranberries | 1/4 cup | 60 mL |
| Cranberry jelly | 1/4 cup | 60 mL |
| Orange juice | 2 tbsp. | 30 mL |

Sprinkle gelatin over first amount of cream in small bowl. Let stand for 1 minute.

Combine second amount of cream and sugar in medium saucepan. Heat and stir on medium until warm and sugar is dissolved. Do not overheat. Remove from heat. Add gelatin mixture. Mix well. Strain into 4 cup (1 L) liquid measure.

Divide custard among four 3/4 cup (175 mL) glasses. Sprinkle with cinnamon. Cool completely. Cover. Chill overnight.

**Rhubarb Compote:** Combine all 4 ingredients in separate medium saucepan. Heat and stir on medium for about 5 minutes until jelly is melted. Reduce heat to medium-low. Simmer, uncovered, for about 10 minutes until thickened. Turn into medium bowl. Cool slightly. Cover. Chill for at least 8 hours or overnight. Makes about 2/3 cup (150 mL) compote. Divide and spoon compote over custards. Serves 4.

1 serving: 304 Calories; 12.9 g Total Fat (3.7 g Mono, 0.5 g Poly, 8 g Sat); 40 mg Cholesterol; 44 g Carbohydrate; 2 g Fibre; 5 g Protein; 60 mg Sodium

Pictured on page 89.

# Crème Caramel

*Easier to make than you would think. These individual servings have a creamy, velvety custard base with the traditional caramel top.*

| | | |
|---|---|---|
| Water | 1 cup | 250 mL |
| Granulated sugar | 1 cup | 250 mL |
| | | |
| Large eggs | 6 | 6 |
| Vanilla | 1 1/2 tsp. | 7 mL |
| Granulated sugar | 1/2 cup | 125 mL |
| | | |
| Homogenized milk | 1 3/4 cups | 425 mL |
| Whipping cream (or homogenized milk) | 1 cup | 250 mL |

Grease eight 1/2 cup (125 mL) ovenproof ramekins. Place in ovenproof pan large enough to hold ramekins.

Combine water and first amount of sugar in medium saucepan (see page 16). Heat and stir on medium for about 3 minutes until sugar is dissolved. Bring to a boil on medium-high. Boil for 5 to 10 minutes, without stirring, until syrup is deep golden brown. Working quickly, divide syrup among ramekins.

Beat eggs, vanilla and second amount of sugar with whisk in large bowl until frothy.

Combine milk and whipping cream in small saucepan. Heat on medium until very hot and bubbles appear around edge. Gradually add hot milk mixture to egg mixture, stirring constantly with whisk, until well combined. Strain into 4 cup (1 L) liquid measure. Divide custard among ramekins. Carefully pour enough boiling water into pan until water comes halfway up sides of ramekins. Bake in 325°F (160°C) oven for about 30 minutes until just set. Remove from water. Cool completely. Cover. Chill for at least 6 hours or overnight. Carefully run knife around inside of each ramekin to loosen. Invert onto 8 individual plates. Serve immediately. Serves 8.

1 serving: 342 Calories; 15.8 g Total Fat (4.9 g Mono, 0.9 g Poly, 8.7 g Sat); 206 mg Cholesterol; 44 g Carbohydrate; 0 g Fibre; 7 g Protein; 87 mg Sodium

Pictured on page 89.

# Honey Cinnamon Rice Custards

*These creamy, comforting desserts have golden brown tops with a smooth cinnamon and honey custard underneath.*

| | | |
|---|---|---|
| Milk | 1 1/2 cups | 375 mL |
| Whipping cream | 1 cup | 250 mL |
| Cinnamon stick (4 inch, 10 cm, length) | 1 | 1 |
| Large eggs | 3 | 3 |
| Granulated sugar | 3 tbsp. | 50 mL |
| Liquid honey | 3 tbsp. | 50 mL |
| Vanilla | 1 tsp. | 5 mL |
| Cooked short grain white rice (about 1/3 cup, 75 mL, uncooked) | 3/4 cup | 175 mL |

Combine first 3 ingredients in small saucepan. Heat on medium until very hot and bubbles appear around edge. Remove from heat. Cover. Let stand for 30 minutes. Remove and discard cinnamon stick.

Add next 4 ingredients to milk mixture. Whisk until well combined and frothy. Pour into 4 cup (1 L) liquid measure.

Divide rice among eight lightly greased 3/4 cup (175 mL) ovenproof ramekins. Place in ovenproof pan large enough to hold ramekins. Divide custard among ramekins. Carefully pour enough boiling water into pan until water comes halfway up sides of ramekins. Bake in 350°F (175°C) oven for about 35 minutes until just set. Serve warm or cold. Serves 8.

1 serving: 214 Calories; 12.5 g Total Fat (3.8 g Mono, 0.6 g Poly, 7.2 g Sat); 119 mg Cholesterol; 21 g Carbohydrate; 0 g Fibre; 5 g Protein; 60 mg Sodium

Pictured on this page.

Top: Rhubarb And Cinnamon Custards, page 88
Centre: Honey Cinnamon Rice Custards, above
Bottom: Crème Caramel, page 88

# Chilled White Chocolate Soup

*This velvety smooth, ivory-coloured "soup" is truly rich and decadent. The delicate, orange liqueur aftertaste blends well with the tart berries and the sweet white chocolate base. The Pecan Crisps add a crunchy complement to this exquisite dessert.*

| | | |
|---|---|---|
| Half-and-half cream | 1 1/4 cups | 300 mL |
| Butter (or hard margarine), melted | 1/4 cup | 60 mL |
| Egg yolk (large), fork-beaten | 1 | 1 |
| White chocolate bars (3 1/2 oz., 100 g, each), chopped | 2 | 2 |
| Whipping cream | 1/2 cup | 125 mL |
| Orange-flavoured liqueur (such as Grand Marnier) | 2 tbsp. | 30 mL |
| **PECAN CRISPS (optional)** | | |
| Large eggs | 2 | 2 |
| Granulated sugar | 2/3 cup | 150 mL |
| Salt | 1/4 tsp. | 1 mL |
| Vanilla | 1/2 tsp. | 2 mL |
| Butter (or hard margarine), melted | 6 tbsp. | 100 mL |
| All-purpose flour | 3/4 cup | 175 mL |
| Egg white (large), fork-beaten | 1 | 1 |
| Finely chopped pecans | 3/4 cup | 175 mL |
| **GARNISH** | | |
| Fresh (or frozen, thawed) berries (your choice) | 1 cup | 250 mL |
| Fresh mint leaves | | |

Heat half-and-half cream and butter in medium saucepan on medium, stirring occasionally, until very hot and bubbles appear around edge. Remove from heat.

Put egg yolk and chocolate into medium bowl. Gradually stir in cream mixture until chocolate is melted. Cool.

Beat whipping cream in small bowl until soft peaks form. Whisk into chocolate mixture.

Add liqueur. Stir. Makes 3 1/3 cups (825 mL) soup. Cover with plastic wrap. Chill for 3 to 4 hours.

**Pecan Crisps:** Grease 11 × 17 inch (28 × 43 cm) baking sheet. Line bottom with parchment (or waxed) paper. Beat first 4 ingredients in separate medium bowl until thickened.

Beat in butter. Add flour. Beat on low until no lumps remain. Spread thinly in prepared pan with offset spatula.

Brush surface well with egg white. Sprinkle with pecans. Bake on centre rack in 350°F (175°C) oven for about 20 minutes until crisp and browned. Immediately cut crosswise into 8 equal strips. Cut each strip in half along length of pan, for a total of 16 rectangles. Cut each rectangle diagonally into triangles. Let stand for about 10 minutes until cool and crisp. Store loosely covered in cool, dry place. Makes 32 crisps.

**Garnish:** Just before serving, whisk soup. Spoon about 1/2 cup (125 mL) into each of 6 shallow dishes or decorative glasses. Arrange a few berries and mint leaves in centre of each soup. Serve with crisps. Serves 6.

1 serving (soup only): 406 Calories; 31.3 g Total Fat (9.4 g Mono, 1.2 g Poly, 18.8 g Sat); 106 mg Cholesterol; 26 g Carbohydrate; 1 g Fibre; 5 g Protein; 144 mg Sodium

3 crisps: 217 Calories; 13.5 g Total Fat (5.9 g Mono, 1.9 g Poly, 4.9 g Sat); 58 mg Cholesterol; 22 g Carbohydrate; 1 g Fibre; 3 g Protein; 149 mg Sodium

Pictured on page 91.

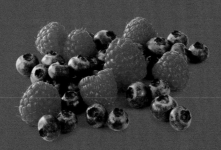

# Crêpes & Blintzes

These delicious, paper-thin desserts enclose a variety
of sweet, satisfying fillings. Drizzle with a warm
fruit sauce, a tempting caramel sauce or a delicately
flavoured liqueur for an elegant presentation
and a taste your guests will love.

## All About Crêpes

The word crêpe (KRAYP) is the French word for pancake. Unlike traditional North American pancakes, crêpes are paper-thin and usually rolled around a sweet or savoury filling. Crêpe batter is made with a combination of simple ingredients: flour, eggs, milk and butter. These luscious, versatile treats can be rolled, folded, stacked, filled, flambéed, or baked and served cold, warm or hot! Read on to learn all about crêpes!

- When making crêpes, dry ingredients are always combined first. Then, wet ingredients are added and mixture is whisked to make batter as smooth as possible. However, whisking action creates air bubbles that need to dissipate before cooking. For this reason, and to allow the flour to swell, the batter must sit for approximately 1 hour before using.

- Always use non-stick pan or pan designed for crêpe preparation. This will prevent batter from sticking to pan, making crêpes easier to flip over.

- To keep crêpes a consistent size, use ladle or measuring cup when adding batter to pan. This will make it easier to judge how much batter to use for each crêpe.

- Add the crêpe batter to hot pan greased with butter. Butter is added regardless of the pan's non-stick properties to add flavour and to aid in browning crêpes.

- When edges start to brown slightly and top appears set, flip crêpe to lightly brown other side. Unlike crêpes, blintzes are only browned on one side and are not flipped.

- When storing crêpes for future use, stack them together, place in sealed container and freeze for up to 1 month. If butter has been used to grease pan, they will not stick, so there is no need to separate crêpes with waxed paper. For same or next day use, stack crêpes, wrap in plastic wrap and place in refrigerator.

## Basic Dessert Crêpes

*These thin, golden brown crêpes can be filled with your choice of delicious ingredients. The batter can easily be doubled to serve a larger group of people.*

| All-purpose flour | 3/4 cup | 175 mL |
| Granulated sugar | 1 tbsp. | 15 mL |
| Salt, just a pinch | | |
| Large eggs, fork-beaten | 2 | 2 |
| Milk | 1 cup | 250 mL |
| Butter (or hard margarine), melted | 3 tbsp. | 50 mL |
| Butter (or hard margarine) | 1 tbsp. | 15 mL |

Combine first 3 ingredients in large bowl. Make a well in centre.

Combine next 3 ingredients in small bowl. Pour into well. Whisk until smooth. Let stand for 1 hour. Stir.

Melt 1/4 tsp. (1 mL) of second amount of butter in 8 inch (20 cm) frying pan on medium. Measure 2 1/2 tbsp. (37 mL) batter into 1/4 cup (60 mL) measure. Pour into pan.

Immediately swirl to coat bottom of pan, lifting and tilting pan to ensure entire bottom is covered.

Cook for 45 to 60 seconds until top is set. Flip. Cook for 45 to 60 seconds until golden brown spots appear on bottom. Remove to plate. Repeat with remaining butter and batter. Makes 12 crêpes.

1 crêpe: 90 Calories; 5 g Total Fat (1.5 g Mono, 0.3 g Poly, 2.8 g Sat); 47 mg Cholesterol; 8 g Carbohydrate; trace Fibre; 3 g Protein; 61 mg Sodium

Pictured on pages 94, 95, 97 and 99.

# Almond Pear Crêpes

*The flavours of almonds and pears go well together—especially when these crêpes are drizzled with the oh-so-sweet sauce.*

### ALMOND CHEESE FILLING

| | | |
|---|---|---|
| Mascarpone cheese (or 4 oz., 125 g, cream cheese, softened) | 1/2 cup | 125 mL |
| Icing (confectioner's) sugar | 2 tbsp. | 30 mL |
| Almond flavouring | 1/4 tsp. | 1 mL |
| Whipping cream | 1/2 cup | 125 mL |
| Sliced almonds, toasted (see Tip, page 20) | 1/4 cup | 60 mL |

### CHOCOLATE BAR SAUCE

| | | |
|---|---|---|
| Evaporated milk (not skim) | 3/4 cup | 175 mL |
| Caramel-filled chocolate bars (3 1/2 oz., 100 g, each), broken into individual squares | 3 | 3 |
| Basic Dessert Crêpes (page 93) | 12 | 12 |
| Cans of pears (14 oz., 398 mL, each), drained well and sliced | 2 | 2 |
| Sliced almonds, toasted | 1/4 cup | 60 mL |

Almond Pear Crêpes, above

**Almond Cheese Filling:** Beat first 3 ingredients in medium bowl until smooth.

Beat whipping cream in small bowl with same beaters until stiff peaks form. Fold into cheese mixture.

Fold in almonds. Makes about 1 cup (250 mL) filling.

**Chocolate Bar Sauce:** Heat evaporated milk in medium saucepan on medium, stirring occasionally, until hot. Reduce heat to low. Add chocolate bar squares. Stir until smooth (see page 17). Makes 1 1/2 cups (375 mL) sauce.

Just before serving, spread about 1 1/2 tbsp. (25 mL) filling down centre of each crêpe. Divide and arrange pear slices on filling. Roll up to enclose filling, leaving ends open. Place 2 filled crêpes on each of 6 individual plates. Drizzle with about 3 tbsp. (50 mL) warm sauce.

Sprinkle with almonds. Makes 12 filled crêpes. Serves 6.

1 serving: 710 Calories; 44.2 g Total Fat (11 g Mono, 2.2 g Poly, 16.5 g Sat); 164 mg Cholesterol; 69 g Carbohydrate; 4 g Fibre; 15 g Protein; 292 mg Sodium

Pictured below.

# Crêpes Suzette

*A delicate, orange liqueur flavour dominates these elegant crêpes. This is a variation of the traditional flambéed crêpes.*

## ORANGE SAUCE

| | | |
|---|---|---|
| Sugar cubes | 12 | 12 |
| Medium navel oranges | 3 | 3 |
| Orange juice | 1 1/2 cups | 375 mL |
| Butter (or hard margarine) | 1/4 cup | 60 mL |
| Orange-flavoured liqueur (such as Grand Marnier) | 3 tbsp. | 50 mL |
| Basic Dessert Crêpes (page 93) | 12 | 12 |

**Orange Sauce:** Rub sugar cubes over skin of oranges until cubes are orange in colour. Place in small plastic bag. Crush with mallet or rolling pin until crumbled. Transfer sugar to large frying pan. Reserve oranges for serving.

Add orange juice. Heat and stir on medium-low until sugar is dissolved. Cook on medium until bubbles appear around edge of frying pan.

Add butter, 1 tbsp. (15 mL) at a time, stirring constantly, until melted.

Add liqueur. Stir. Bring to a gentle boil. Boil for 3 minutes to blend flavours. Makes about 1 1/2 cups (375 mL) sauce.

Fold crêpes into quarters to form triangles. Arrange 3 folded crêpes, overlapping slightly, on each of 4 individual plates. Drizzle each with about 6 tbsp. (100 mL) sauce. Peel reserved oranges. Cut into segments. Divide and arrange on sauce. Serve warm. Serves 4.

1 serving: 524 Calories; 27.7 g Total Fat (8.1 g Mono, 1.4 g Poly, 16.2 g Sat); 175 mg Cholesterol; 55 g Carbohydrate; 1 g Fibre; 10 g Protein; 310 mg Sodium

Pictured below.

Crêpes Suzette, above

# Apple Crêpe Cake

*This multi-layered crêpe dessert is sweet and so delicious! The apple-cinnamon-raisin flavour is complemented by the smooth caramel sauce.*

## APPLE FILLING

| | | |
|---|---|---|
| Butter (or hard margarine) | 3 tbsp. | 50 mL |
| Golden raisins | 2/3 cup | 150 mL |
| Ground cinnamon | 1/2 tsp. | 2 mL |
| Tart medium cooking apples (such as Granny Smith), peeled, quartered and thinly sliced | 6 | 6 |
| Brown sugar, packed | 1/4 cup | 60 mL |
| Basic Dessert Crêpes (page 93) | 12 | 12 |

## ANISE CARAMEL SAUCE

| | | |
|---|---|---|
| Brown sugar, packed | 2/3 cup | 150 mL |
| Whipping cream | 2/3 cup | 150 mL |
| Butter (or hard margarine) | 1/2 cup | 125 mL |
| Star anise (or 1/16 tsp., 0.5 mL, ground anise) | 1 | 1 |
| Brandy (optional) | 1 tbsp. | 15 mL |

**Apple Filling:** Heat first 3 ingredients in large frying pan on medium-high, stirring constantly, until butter is melted.

Add apple and brown sugar. Stir. Cook for 5 minutes, stirring occasionally. Reduce heat to medium. Cook for about 5 minutes until apple is tender. Cool.

Place 1 crêpe on large flat plate. Divide filling into 11 portions. Spread 1 portion on crêpe. Place another crêpe on top. Repeat layers with remaining crêpes and filling, ending with crêpe layer. Cover. Invert large plate over top of crêpe stack. Weigh top down with unopened 14 oz. (398 mL) can. Chill overnight.

**Anise Caramel Sauce:** Combine all 5 ingredients in medium saucepan. Heat and stir on medium until butter is melted and brown sugar is dissolved. Bring to a boil. Boil gently for about 5 minutes, without stirring, until thickened slightly. Makes about 1 1/4 cups (300 mL) sauce. Remove and discard star anise. Drizzle cake with 1/2 of sauce. Just before serving, cut cake with serrated knife. Warm remaining sauce. Drizzle over individual servings. Serves 6.

1 serving: 719 Calories; 41.6 g Total Fat (12.1 g Mono, 1.8 g Poly, 25.1 g Sat); 187 mg Cholesterol; 85 g Carbohydrate; 4 g Fibre; 7 g Protein; 373 mg Sodium

Pictured on page 97.

# Banana Rum Crêpes

*These sweet cinnamon crêpes have a soft banana filling. The drizzle of dark, rich sauce creates an impressive finishing touch.*

## CINNAMON CRÊPE BATTER

| | | |
|---|---|---|
| Basic Dessert Crêpe batter (page 93) | | |
| Ground cinnamon | 1/2 tsp. | 2 mL |

## BANANA RUM FILLING

| | | |
|---|---|---|
| Butter (or hard margarine) | 3 tbsp. | 50 mL |
| Brown sugar, packed | 3 tbsp. | 50 mL |
| Spiced rum | 2 tbsp. | 30 mL |
| Sliced banana (about 4 medium) | 3 cups | 750 mL |
| Finely chopped crystallized ginger | 2 tbsp. | 30 mL |

Chocolate Bar Sauce (page 94), optional

**Cinnamon Crêpe Batter:** Add cinnamon to dry ingredients of Basic Dessert Crêpe batter. Prepare as directed. Makes 12 crêpes.

**Banana Rum Filling:** Heat butter and brown sugar in large frying pan on medium, stirring constantly, until butter is melted and brown sugar is dissolved.

Add rum. Carefully ignite with match.

Add banana and ginger. Stir. Cook for about 2 minutes, stirring occasionally, until banana is hot and softened slightly. Makes 2 cups (500 mL) filling.

Divide and spoon filling down centre of each crêpe. Roll up to enclose filling, leaving ends open. Arrange on large platter. Drizzle sauce over crêpes. Makes 12 filled crêpes.

1 filled crêpe: 172 Calories; 8.1 g Total Fat (2.4 g Mono, 0.4 g Poly, 4.7 g Sat); 55 mg Cholesterol; 22 g Carbohydrate; 1 g Fibre; 3 g Protein; 93 mg Sodium

Pictured on page 97.

Upper Right: Banana Rum Crêpes, above
Bottom: Apple Crêpe Cake, this page

# Apple-Filled Hazelnut Crêpes

*The tart apple filling and the sweet, nutty batter go very well together.*

### HAZELNUT CRÊPES

| | | |
|---|---|---|
| All-purpose flour | 1 1/2 cups | 375 mL |
| Granulated sugar | 2 tbsp. | 30 mL |
| Salt, just a pinch | | |
| Large eggs, fork-beaten | 4 | 4 |
| Milk | 2 cups | 500 mL |
| Butter (or hard margarine), melted | 1/3 cup | 75 mL |
| Hazelnuts (filberts), toasted (see Tip, page 20) and finely chopped | 2/3 cup | 150 mL |
| Butter (or hard margarine) | 2 tbsp. | 30 mL |

### APPLE MAPLE FILLING

| | | |
|---|---|---|
| Butter (or hard margarine) | 1/2 cup | 125 mL |
| Sliced tart cooking apple (such as Granny Smith) | 8 cups | 2 L |
| Maple (or maple-flavoured) syrup | 1/2 cup | 125 mL |

Icing (confectioner's) sugar, for dusting

**Hazelnut Crêpes:** Combine first 3 ingredients in large bowl. Make a well in centre.

Combine next 3 ingredients in medium bowl. Pour into well. Whisk until smooth. Let stand for 1 hour.

Add hazelnuts. Stir.

Melt 1/2 tsp. (2 mL) of second amount of butter in 12 inch (30 cm) non-stick frying pan on medium. Pour 1/3 cup (75 mL) batter into pan. Immediately swirl to coat bottom of pan, lifting and tilting pan to ensure entire bottom is covered. Cook for 45 to 60 seconds until top is set. Flip. Cook for 45 to 60 seconds until golden brown spots appear on bottom. Remove to plate. Repeat with remaining butter and batter, stirring batter in bowl each time to distribute hazelnuts. Makes 12 crêpes.

**Apple Maple Filling:** Melt butter in same frying pan on medium. Add apple slices. Cook for about 10 minutes, stirring occasionally, until starting to soften.

Add maple syrup. Stir. Cook for 5 to 10 minutes, stirring occasionally, until apple slices are soft, but not broken down.

Divide and spoon filling onto 1/4 of each crêpe. Fold crêpes over to form triangles. Arrange on platter. Dust with icing sugar just before serving. Makes 12 filled crêpes.

*1 filled crêpe: 385 Calories; 22.9 g Total Fat (8.8 g Mono, 1.4 g Poly, 11.2 g Sat); 117 mg Cholesterol; 41 g Carbohydrate; 3 g Fibre; 7 g Protein; 208 mg Sodium*

Pictured on page 99.

# Soufflé Crêpes

*These golden crêpes have a light, fluffy filling and are served with fresh, seasonal berries.*

### BERRY TOPPING

| | | |
|---|---|---|
| Strawberry jam | 1/4 cup | 60 mL |
| Orange juice | 1/3 cup | 75 mL |
| Orange-flavoured liqueur (such as Grand Marnier), optional | 1 tbsp. | 15 mL |
| Chopped fresh strawberries (see Note) | 2 cups | 500 mL |
| Fresh raspberries | 1 cup | 250 mL |
| Fresh blueberries | 1 cup | 250 mL |

### CUSTARD FILLING

| | | |
|---|---|---|
| Milk | 1 cup | 250 mL |
| Vanilla | 1/2 tsp. | 2 mL |
| Granulated sugar | 2/3 cup | 150 mL |
| Egg yolks (large) | 4 | 4 |
| Cornstarch | 2 tbsp. | 30 mL |
| Egg whites (large), room temperature | 4 | 4 |
| Basic Dessert Crêpes (page 93) | 12 | 12 |

**Berry Topping:** Combine first 3 ingredients in small saucepan. Heat and stir on medium-high until jam is dissolved. Boil for about 5 minutes, without stirring, until slightly thickened. Pour into large bowl. Cool.

Add next 3 ingredients. Stir. Cover. Chill until ready to use. Stir just before serving. Makes about 2 1/2 cups (625 mL) topping.

**Custard Filling:** Combine milk and vanilla in medium saucepan. Heat on medium-high until small bubbles appear around edge of saucepan. Remove from heat.

Beat sugar and egg yolks in separate large bowl until thick and pale.

Add cornstarch. Stir until smooth. Whisk milk mixture into egg yolk mixture. Return to same saucepan. Heat and stir on medium for about 5 minutes until thickened. Turn into separate large bowl. Cover. Cool.

Beat egg whites in medium bowl until stiff (not dry) peaks form. Fold, in 2 batches, into cooled custard. Makes 2 1/2 cups (625 mL) filling.

Working quickly, divide and spoon filling onto 1/2 of each crêpe. Fold over to cover filling. Place on greased baking sheets. Bake in 350°F (175°C) oven for 10 to 15 minutes until filling is puffed and cooked. Serve with topping. Makes 12 filled crêpes.

1 filled crêpe (with topping): 217 Calories; 7.2 g Total Fat (2.3 g Mono, 0.6 g Poly, 3.5 g Sat); 120 mg Cholesterol; 33 g Carbohydrate; 2 g Fibre; 6 g Protein; 97 mg Sodium

Pictured below.

**Note:** If fresh fruit isn't available, use well-drained frozen fruit.

Top Left: Apple-Filled Hazelnut Crêpes, page 98

Bottom: Soufflé Crêpes, page 98

# Banana Toffee Crêpes

*It doesn't get much more decadent than toffee, chocolate, bananas and cream! This rich dessert is very pretty—perfect for that special occasion.*

### BUTTERSCOTCH CRÊPES

| | | |
|---|---|---|
| All-purpose flour | 3/4 cup | 175 mL |
| Brown sugar, packed | 1 tbsp. | 15 mL |
| Ground cinnamon | 1/4 tsp. | 1 mL |
| Salt, just a pinch | | |
| Large eggs, fork-beaten | 2 | 2 |
| Milk | 1 cup | 250 mL |
| Butter (or hard margarine), melted | 3 tbsp. | 50 mL |
| Butter (or hard margarine) | 1 tbsp. | 15 mL |

| | | |
|---|---|---|
| Whipping cream | 1 1/2 cups | 375 mL |
| Icing (confectioner's) sugar | 3 tbsp. | 50 mL |
| Vanilla | 1/2 tsp. | 2 mL |
| Chocolate-covered crispy toffee bars (such as Skor), 1 1/2 oz. (39 g}, each | 6 | 6 |
| Medium bananas, diced | 3 | 3 |
| Caramel (or butterscotch) ice cream topping | 1/4 cup | 60 mL |
| Chocolate (or fudge) ice cream topping | 1/4 cup | 60 mL |

**Butterscotch Crêpes:** Combine first 4 ingredients in large bowl. Make a well in centre.

Apricot Blintzes, page 102

Combine next 3 ingredients in small bowl. Pour into well. Whisk until smooth. Let stand for 1 hour. Stir.

Melt 1/4 tsp. (1 mL) of second amount of butter in 8 inch (20 cm) frying pan on medium. Measure 2 1/2 tbsp. (37 mL) batter into 1/4 cup (60 mL) measure. Pour into pan. Immediately swirl to coat bottom of pan, lifting and tilting pan to ensure entire bottom is covered. Cook for 45 to 60 seconds until top is set. Flip. Cook for 45 to 60 seconds until golden brown spots appear on bottom. Remove to plate. Repeat with remaining butter and batter. Makes 12 crêpes.

Beat whipping cream, icing sugar and vanilla in separate large bowl until stiff peaks form.

Place toffee bars in large plastic bag. Crush with mallet or rolling pin until coarse crumbs. Reserve 1/2 cup (125 mL). Fold remaining crumbs and banana into whipped cream. Makes 5 cups (1.25 L) filling. Spoon generous 1/3 cup (75 mL) filling down centre of each crêpe. Roll up to enclose filling, leaving ends open. Place 2 filled crêpes on each of 6 individual plates.

Drizzle caramel and chocolate toppings over crêpes using squeeze bottle or piping bag (see page 176) with small hole for the tip. Sprinkle with reserved toffee bar crumbs. Makes 12 filled crêpes. Serves 6.

1 serving: 735 Calories; 46 g Total Fat (9.5 g Mono, 1.8 g Poly, 19.3 g Sat); 193 mg Cholesterol; 76 g Carbohydrate; 2 g Fibre; 10 g Protein; 307 mg Sodium

Pictured below.

Banana Toffee Crêpes, page 100

# Apricot Blintzes

*These warm, inviting blintzes have a buttery flavour with a hint of cinnamon. The tart sauce adds a touch of colour and a pleasing contrast to the mellow filling.*

| | | |
|---|---|---|
| All-purpose flour | 1 cup | 250 mL |
| Granulated sugar | 1 tbsp. | 15 mL |
| Salt, just a pinch | | |
| | | |
| Large eggs, fork-beaten | 3 | 3 |
| Milk | 1 cup | 250 mL |
| Butter (or hard margarine), melted | 2 tbsp. | 30 mL |
| | | |
| Butter (or hard margarine) | 1 tbsp. | 15 mL |

**CREAM CHEESE FILLING**

| | | |
|---|---|---|
| Finely chopped apricots | 1/2 cup | 125 mL |
| Brandy | 1 1/2 tbsp. | 25 mL |
| | | |
| Blocks of cream cheese (8 oz., 250 g, each), softened | 2 | 2 |
| Sour cream | 1/3 cup | 75 mL |
| Large egg | 1 | 1 |
| Granulated sugar | 1/3 cup | 75 mL |
| Ground cinnamon | 1/2 tsp. | 2 mL |
| | | |
| Butter (or hard margarine) | 2 tbsp. | 30 mL |
| Cooking oil | 1 tbsp. | 15 mL |

**APRICOT SAUCE**

| | | |
|---|---|---|
| Apricot nectar | 1 cup | 250 mL |
| Apricot jam | 1/3 cup | 75 mL |

Combine first 3 ingredients in large bowl. Make a well in centre.

Combine next 3 ingredients in small bowl. Pour into well. Whisk until smooth. Let stand for 1 hour. Stir.

Melt 1/4 tsp. (1 mL) of second amount of butter in 9 1/2 inch (24 cm) frying pan on medium. Measure 3 tbsp. (50 mL) batter into 1/4 cup (60 mL) measure. Pour into pan. Immediately swirl to coat bottom of pan, lifting and tilting pan to ensure entire bottom is covered. Cook for 45 to 60 seconds until top is set. Do not flip. Remove to plate. Repeat with remaining butter and batter. Makes 12 crêpes.

**Cream Cheese Filling:** Combine apricots and brandy in small bowl.

Beat next 5 ingredients in large bowl until smooth. Add apricot mixture. Stir. Cover. Chill for at least 6 hours or overnight. Makes 3 cups (750 mL) filling. Spoon 1/4 cup (60 mL) filling in centre, on uncooked side, of each crêpe. Fold sides of each crêpe around filling to make rectangular parcel.

Heat butter and cooking oil in large frying pan on medium. Add parcels, seam-side down. Cook for about 1 minute per side until golden brown. Remove to paper towels.

**Apricot Sauce:** Combine nectar and jam in medium saucepan. Heat and stir on medium-high until jam is dissolved. Boil for 5 to 10 minutes, without stirring, until thickened. Remove from heat. Makes 3/4 cup (175 mL) sauce. Arrange 2 blintzes on each of 6 individual plates. Divide and drizzle sauce over top. Makes 12 blintzes. Serves 6.

1 serving: 704 Calories; 47.1 g Total Fat (14.4 g Mono, 2.7 g Poly, 27.1 g Sat); 268 mg Cholesterol; 56 g Carbohydrate; 1 g Fibre; 15 g Protein; 424 mg Sodium

Pictured on page 100.

# Creamy Cherry Blintzes

*These golden brown parcels have a sweet, creamy filling and dark, sweet sauce.*

| | | |
|---|---|---|
| All-purpose flour | 1 cup | 250 mL |
| Granulated sugar | 1 tbsp. | 15 mL |
| Salt, just a pinch | | |
| | | |
| Large eggs, fork-beaten | 3 | 3 |
| Milk | 1 cup | 250 mL |
| Butter (or hard margarine), melted | 2 tbsp. | 30 mL |
| | | |
| Butter (or hard margarine) | 1 tbsp. | 15 mL |

**CREAM CHEESE FILLING**

| | | |
|---|---|---|
| Sultana raisins | 1/2 cup | 125 mL |
| Boiling water, to cover | | |
| | | |
| Blocks of cream cheese (8 oz., 250 g, each), softened | 2 | 2 |
| Sour cream | 1/3 cup | 75 mL |
| Large egg | 1 | 1 |
| Granulated sugar | 1/3 cup | 75 mL |
| Finely grated lemon zest | 2 tsp. | 10 mL |
| | | |
| Butter (or hard margarine) | 2 tbsp. | 30 mL |
| Cooking oil | 1 tbsp. | 15 mL |

## CHERRY SAUCE

| | | |
|---|---|---|
| Can of pitted Bing cherries (with juice) | 14 oz. | 398 mL |
| Cherry jam | 1/2 cup | 125 mL |
| Cherry-flavoured liqueur (such as Kirsch), optional | 2 tbsp. | 30 mL |

Combine first 3 ingredients in large bowl. Make a well in centre.

Combine next 3 ingredients in small bowl. Pour into well. Whisk until smooth. Let stand for 1 hour. Stir.

Melt 1/4 tsp. (1 mL) of second amount of butter in 9 1/2 inch (24 cm) frying pan on medium. Measure 3 tbsp. (50 mL) batter into 1/4 cup (60 mL) measure. Pour into pan. Immediately swirl to coat bottom of pan, lifting and tilting pan to ensure entire bottom is covered. Cook for 45 to 60 seconds until top is set. Do not flip. Remove to plate. Repeat with remaining butter and batter. Makes 12 crêpes.

**Cream Cheese Filling:** Put raisins into small bowl. Cover with boiling water. Let stand for 30 minutes. Drain.

Beat next 5 ingredients in large bowl until smooth. Add raisins. Stir. Makes 3 cups (750 mL) filling. Spoon 1/4 cup (60 mL) filling in centre, on uncooked side of each crêpe. Fold sides of each crêpe around filling to make rectangular parcel.

Heat butter and cooking oil in large frying pan on medium. Add parcels, seam-side down. Cook for about 1 minute per side until golden brown. Remove to paper towels.

**Cherry Sauce:** Drain juice from cherries into medium saucepan. Halve cherries. Set aside. Add jam and liqueur to juice. Heat and stir on medium-high until jam is dissolved. Boil for 5 to 10 minutes, without stirring, until thickened. Remove from heat. Add cherries. Stir. Makes 1 1/2 cups (375 mL) sauce. Arrange 2 blintzes on each of 6 individual plates. Divide and spoon sauce over blintzes. Makes 12 blintzes. Serves 6.

1 serving: 763 Calories; 47.1 g Total Fat (14.4 g Mono, 2.8 g Poly, 27.1 g Sat); 268 mg Cholesterol; 74 g Carbohydrate; 2 g Fibre; 16 g Protein; 430 mg Sodium

Pictured below.

# Frozen Desserts

An ice-cold, refreshing dessert from your freezer may be
exactly what your guests are looking for. This special collection
of recipes, with its variety of fresh and exciting flavours,
can turn a warm day into a cool feast.

# Black Forest Sundaes

*These eye-catching sundaes are covered in a rich cherry and chocolate sauce. Serve in tall sundae glasses for that old-fashioned "ice cream shoppe" feel.*

CHERRY SAUCE

| | | |
|---|---|---|
| Can of pitted Bing cherries (with juice) | 14 oz. | 398 mL |
| Granulated sugar | 2 tbsp. | 30 mL |
| Lemon juice | 1 1/2 tsp. | 7 mL |
| Cornstarch | 2 tsp. | 10 mL |

CHOCOLATE SAUCE

| | | |
|---|---|---|
| Semi-sweet chocolate baking squares (1 oz., 28 g, each), chopped | 4 | 4 |
| Whipping cream | 1/4 cup | 60 mL |
| Scoops of chocolate ice cream | 6 | 6 |
| Scoops of vanilla ice cream | 6 | 6 |

GARNISH

| | | |
|---|---|---|
| Whipped cream | 1/2 cup | 125 mL |
| Hazelnuts (filberts), toasted (see Tip, page 20) and chopped | 3 tbsp. | 50 mL |
| Maraschino cherries (with stems), drained | 6 | 6 |

**Cherry Sauce:** Drain juice from cherries into medium saucepan. Set cherries aside.

Add next 3 ingredients to juice. Heat and stir on medium for 5 to 10 minutes until hot and thickened. Add cherries. Stir until coated. Remove from heat. Cool slightly. Makes 1 3/4 cups (425 mL) sauce.

**Chocolate Sauce:** Combine chocolate and whipping cream in small heavy saucepan. Heat and stir on medium-low until chocolate is almost melted. Do not overheat. Remove from heat. Stir until smooth. Cool slightly. Makes 2/3 cup (150 mL) sauce.

Put 1 scoop of chocolate and 1 scoop vanilla ice cream into each of 6 individual sundae glasses. Drizzle each with about 1/4 cup (60 mL) Cherry Sauce, then with about 1 1/2 tbsp. (25 mL) Chocolate Sauce.

**Garnish:** Dollop with whipped cream. Sprinkle with hazelnuts. Top each with maraschino cherry. Serves 6.

1 serving: 470 Calories; 24.4 g Total Fat (7.3 g Mono, 0.9 g Poly, 14.9 g Sat); 67 mg Cholesterol; 63 g Carbohydrate; 2 g Fibre; 7 g Protein; 117 mg Sodium

Pictured on this page.

# Layered Gelato Cake

*This is a very striking cake!*
*A layer of miniature jelly rolls is topped with*
*tart mango and raspberry gelato. The fresh flavours,*
*colours and textures complement each other beautifully.*

| | | |
|---|---|---|
| Packages of jam-filled jelly rolls (such as Swiss rolls), 3/4 lb. (340 g) each (6 per package) | 2 | 2 |
| Raspberry jam | 1/2 cup | 125 mL |
| **MANGO GELATO** | | |
| Granulated sugar | 1/2 cup | 125 mL |
| Unflavoured gelatin | 1 1/2 tsp. | 7 mL |
| Salt, sprinkle | | |
| Half-and-half cream | 1 1/4 cups | 300 mL |
| Can of sliced mango, drained | 14 oz. | 398 mL |
| Egg white (large), room temperature | 1 | 1 |
| **RASPBERRY GELATO** | | |
| Granulated sugar | 1/2 cup | 125 mL |
| Unflavoured gelatin | 1 1/2 tsp. | 7 mL |
| Salt, sprinkle | | |
| Half-and-half cream | 1 1/4 cups | 300 mL |
| Fresh (or whole frozen, thawed, with juice) raspberries | 2 1/2 cups | 625 mL |
| Egg white (large), room temperature | 1 | 1 |
| Fresh raspberries, for garnish | | |

Cut each jelly roll into 3/4 inch (2 cm) slices. Reserve 14 slices. Fit remaining slices, cut side down, in bottom of ungreased 10 inch (25 cm) springform pan. Arrange reserved slices around inside edge of pan. Spoon jam over bottom layer. Spread evenly to cover completely. Freeze.

**Mango Gelato:** Combine sugar, gelatin and salt in small saucepan. Add cream. Heat and stir on medium for 3 to 4 minutes until sugar and gelatin are dissolved completely. Cool slightly.

Purée mango in blender or food processor. Add to gelatin mixture. Stir.

Beat egg white in medium bowl until soft peaks form. Fold mango mixture into egg white. Spread evenly in ungreased 9 x 9 inch (22 x 22 cm) pan. Freeze, uncovered, for about 1 hour until slushy. Transfer to separate medium bowl. Beat on high until foamy and light. Makes about 2 1/4 cups (550 mL) Mango Gelato. Spread evenly over jam. Cover. Freeze for 2 hours.

**Raspberry Gelato:** Combine sugar, gelatin and salt in small saucepan. Add cream. Heat and stir on medium for 3 to 4 minutes until sugar and gelatin are dissolved completely. Cool slightly.

Purée first amount of raspberries in blender or food processor. Put through food mill or sieve to remove seeds. Discard seeds. You should have about 1 cup (250 mL) raspberry purée. Add to gelatin mixture. Stir.

Beat egg white in medium bowl until soft peaks form. Fold raspberry mixture into egg white. Spread evenly in separate ungreased 9 x 9 inch (22 x 22 cm) pan. Freeze, uncovered, for about 1 hour until slushy. Transfer to separate medium bowl. Beat on high until foamy and light. Makes about 2 cups (500 mL) Raspberry Gelato. Spread evenly over mango layer. Cover. Freeze for at least 8 hours or overnight until firm. Let stand at room temperature for 30 minutes, or in refrigerator for 1 hour, before cutting.

Garnish with second amount of raspberries. Cuts into 12 wedges.

1 wedge: 358 Calories; 6.8 g Total Fat (2 g Mono, 0.5 g Poly, 3.7 g Sat); 63 mg Cholesterol; 71 g Carbohydrate; 2 g Fibre; 6 g Protein; 155 mg Sodium

Pictured on page 107.

# Peppermint Ice Cream

*This smooth, green ice cream is topped with a rich chocolate sauce. The kids will devour this dreamy dessert!*

| | | |
|---|---|---|
| Egg yolks (large) | 4 | 4 |
| Granulated sugar | 1/2 cup | 125 mL |
| Milk | 2 cups | 500 mL |
| Whipping cream | 2 cups | 500 mL |
| Drops of green food colouring | 1 – 2 | 1 – 2 |
| Peppermint flavouring | 1 tsp. | 5 mL |
| CHOCOLATE SAUCE | | |
| Milk chocolate bars (3 1/2 oz., 100 g, each), chopped | 2 | 2 |
| Whipping cream | 1/2 cup | 125 mL |
| Large white marshmallows, chopped | 4 | 4 |

Chocolate Filigrees (page 177), for garnish

Beat egg yolks and sugar in medium bowl until pale and thickened.

Heat milk and whipping cream in medium saucepan on medium until bubbles form around edge of saucepan. Gradually whisk into egg yolk mixture. Return to same saucepan. Heat and stir on medium for 5 to 10 minutes until thickened and coats back of metal spoon. Pour into large bowl.

Add food colouring and peppermint flavouring. Stir. Cover with plastic wrap. Chill for at least 3 hours until cold. Pour into ice-cream maker. Freeze according to manufacturer's instructions. Spoon into ungreased 9 x 9 inch (22 x 22 cm) pan. Smooth top. Cover. Freeze overnight until firm. Makes 3 cups (750 mL) ice cream.

**Chocolate Sauce:** Combine first 3 ingredients in small saucepan. Heat and stir on lowest heat until chocolate is melted and marshmallow is dissolved. Makes 1 1/3 cups (325 mL) sauce.

Divide and scoop ice cream into 6 individual bowls. Drizzle with warm sauce. Garnish with filigrees. Serves 6.

1 serving: 648 Calories; 48.2 g Total Fat (14.8 g Mono, 1.9 g Poly, 28.8 g Sat); 276 mg Cholesterol; 49 g Carbohydrate; 1 g Fibre; 9 g Protein; 115 mg Sodium

Pictured on page 109.

# Strawberry Ice Cream

*Beautiful strawberry red swirls flow throughout vanilla ice cream. When drizzled with the sweet strawberry sauce and served in tuile baskets (page 178), this is truly a decadent dessert.*

| | | |
|---|---|---|
| Vanilla ice cream, softened | 4 cups | 1 L |
| Chopped fresh strawberries | 1 cup | 250 mL |
| Strawberry ice cream topping | 3/4 cup | 175 mL |
| STRAWBERRY SAUCE | | |
| Chopped fresh strawberries | 1 1/2 cups | 375 mL |
| Strawberry ice cream topping | 1/4 cup | 60 mL |
| Orange-flavoured liqueur (such as Grand Marnier) or orange juice | 3 tbsp. | 50 mL |
| Granulated sugar | 2 tbsp. | 30 mL |
| Water | 2 tbsp. | 30 mL |

Spoon ice cream into ungreased 8 x 8 inch (20 x 20 cm) pan. Spread evenly. Swirl strawberries and topping through ice cream. Cover. Freeze for at least 6 hours or overnight until firm. Scoop into 8 large balls or 16 smaller ones. Place on ungreased baking sheet. Return to freezer until ready to serve.

**Strawberry Sauce:** Combine all 5 ingredients in large frying pan. Heat and stir on medium until sugar is dissolved. Bring to a boil on medium-high. Boil for about 5 minutes, without stirring, until slightly thickened. Cool. Makes about 1 1/3 cups (325 mL) sauce. Just before serving, put 1 large ice cream ball or 2 smaller balls into each of 8 individual bowls (or tuile baskets, see pages 178 and 179). Divide and drizzle sauce over ice cream. Serves 8.

1 serving: 295 Calories; 7.9 g Total Fat (2.2 g Mono, 0.4 g Poly, 4.8 g Sat); 31 mg Cholesterol; 53 g Carbohydrate; 1 g Fibre; 3 g Protein; 66 mg Sodium

Pictured on page 109.

Top: Peppermint Ice Cream, this page
Bottom: Strawberry Ice Cream, above

# Peach Gelato

*Refreshing scoops of this peach gelato sit in delicate orange blossom bowls. Serve immediately out of the freezer as the bowls will only keep their shape for about 15 minutes.*

| | | |
|---|---|---|
| Granulated sugar | 1/3 cup | 75 mL |
| Unflavoured gelatin | 1 1/2 tsp. | 7 mL |
| Salt | 1/8 tsp. | 0.5 mL |
| Half-and-half cream | 1 1/4 cups | 300 mL |
| Can of sliced peaches (or 1 cup, 250 mL, frozen, thawed), drained | 14 oz. | 398 mL |
| Peach schnapps (or peach brandy), optional | 2 tbsp. | 30 mL |
| Egg white (large), room temperature | 1 | 1 |

### ORANGE BLOSSOM BOWLS (optional)

| | | |
|---|---|---|
| Granulated sugar | 1/2 cup | 125 mL |
| Water | 1/2 cup | 125 mL |
| Medium navel oranges | 5 – 6 | 5 – 6 |

**Fresh mint leaves, for garnish**

Combine sugar, gelatin and salt in small saucepan. Add cream. Heat and stir on medium for 3 to 4 minutes until sugar and gelatin are dissolved completely. Cool slightly.

Purée peach slices in blender or food processor. Add to gelatin mixture. Add schnapps. Stir.

Beat egg white in medium bowl until soft peaks form. Fold peach mixture into egg white. Spread evenly in ungreased 9 x 9 inch (22 x 22 cm) pan. Freeze, uncovered, for about 1 hour until slushy. Transfer to separate medium bowl. Beat on high for about 2 minutes until foamy and light. Spread in same pan. Cover. Freeze for at least 8 hours or overnight until firm. Makes about 2 1/2 cups (625 mL) gelato.

**Orange Blossom Bowls:** Combine sugar and water in small saucepan (see page 16). Bring to a boil on high. Reduce heat to medium-low. Simmer for 5 minutes, stirring occasionally. Cool slightly. Chill until cold.

Cut oranges crosswise into 1/16 inch (1.5 mm) slices with very sharp knife or mandoline. They must be very thin to form bowl shape.

Line 10 fruit nappies or small dessert bowls with plastic wrap. Using only nicest orange slices, dip 1 at a time, into sugar syrup and arrange, overlapping, around side of prepared fruit nappies. Lay 1 orange slice flat on bottom in each (see Note). Cover with plastic wrap, pressing down against fruit. Freeze for several hours or overnight until firm. Unwrap and remove bowls. Peel off and discard plastic wrap. Keep frozen until ready to serve. Makes 10 bowls.

Scoop small balls of gelato into frozen orange bowls. Garnish with mint leaves. Serves 10.

1 serving (without bowl): 74 Calories; 3.2 g Total Fat (0.9 g Mono, 0.1 g Poly, 2 g Sat); 10 mg Cholesterol; 10 g Carbohydrate; trace Fibre; 2 g Protein; 51 mg Sodium

Pictured on page 111.

**Note:** There may be some sugar syrup and orange slices left over. Use in punch or other beverage or serve with ice cream.

**To Make Ahead:** Freeze orange bowls in airtight container for up to 10 days.

# Ice Cream And Mud Cake

*The dense, fudge-like cake goes so well with the vanilla ice cream. The subtle hint of orange liqueur adds a richness to the overall flavour that is just beyond compare!*

### VANILLA ICE CREAM

| | | |
|---|---|---|
| Vanilla bean (or 1 tsp., 5 mL, vanilla) | 1 | 1 |
| Homogenized milk | 2 2/3 cups | 650 mL |
| Egg yolks (large) | 6 | 6 |
| Granulated sugar | 3/4 cup | 175 mL |
| Whipping cream | 1 cup | 250 mL |

### PECAN MUD CAKE

| | | |
|---|---|---|
| Butter (or hard margarine), cut up | 1 cup | 250 mL |
| Semi-sweet chocolate baking squares (1 oz., 28 g, each), chopped | 8 | 8 |
| Water | 3/4 cup | 175 mL |
| Brown sugar, packed | 1 cup | 250 mL |
| Finely grated orange zest | 2 tsp. | 10 mL |
| All-purpose flour | 1 cup | 250 mL |
| Baking powder | 1/2 tsp. | 2 mL |
| Cocoa, sifted if lumpy | 1/3 cup | 75 mL |
| Large eggs, fork-beaten | 2 | 2 |
| Orange-flavoured liqueur (such as Grand Marnier) | 1/4 cup | 60 mL |
| Pecans, toasted (see Tip, page 20) and chopped | 1/2 cup | 125 mL |

### FUDGE SAUCE

| | | |
|---|---|---|
| Semi-sweet chocolate baking squares (1 oz., 28 g, each), chopped | 8 | 8 |
| Whipping cream | 2/3 cup | 150 mL |
| Large white marshmallows, quartered | 8 | 8 |
| Pecans, toasted (see Tip, page 20) and chopped, for garnish | | |

**Vanilla Ice Cream:** Split vanilla bean in half lengthwise. Scrape seeds from pod. Put seeds, pod and milk into medium saucepan. Stir. Bring to a boil. Remove from heat. Cover. Let stand for 15 minutes. Remove and discard seeds and pod.

Beat egg yolks and sugar in large bowl until well combined. Bring milk mixture to a boil. Reduce heat to medium-low. Gradually whisk in egg yolk mixture. Heat and stir for 5 to 10 minutes until thickened and coats back of metal spoon. Pour into separate large bowl. Cover with plastic wrap. Chill for at least 3 hours until cold.

Beat whipping cream in small bowl until soft peaks form. Fold into custard. Pour into ice-cream maker. Freeze according to manufacturer's instructions. Spoon into ungreased 9 × 9 inch (22 × 22 cm) pan. Smooth top. Cover. Freeze overnight until firm. Makes 5 cups (1.25 L) ice cream.

**Pecan Mud Cake:** Line 9 inch (22 cm) springform pan with foil. Heat first 5 ingredients in large saucepan on medium for about 5 minutes until chocolate is almost melted. Do not overheat. Remove from heat. Stir until smooth. Cool slightly.

Add next 5 ingredients. Whisk until smooth.

Add pecans. Stir. Pour into prepared pan. Spread evenly. Bake in 325°F (160°C) oven for about 1 hour until almost set. Centre may still be soft when tested with wooden pick, but will set upon cooling. Let stand in pan on wire rack until cooled completely. Do not remove from pan. Cover. Chill overnight.

**Fudge Sauce:** Combine first 3 ingredients in medium saucepan. Heat and stir on lowest heat for 5 to 7 minutes until chocolate is melted and marshmallow is dissolved. Makes about 1 1/2 cups (375 mL) sauce.

Just before serving, remove cake from pan. Cut cake into 24 thin wedges. Put 1 large or 2 small scoops of ice cream onto each of 12 individual plates. Arrange 2 wedges of cake on each plate beside ice cream. Divide and drizzle warm sauce over cake and ice cream. Sprinkle with pecans. Serves 12.

1 serving: 738 Calories; 47.9 g Total Fat (15.9 g Mono, 2.8 g Poly, 26.5 g Sat); 236 mg Cholesterol; 74 g Carbohydrate; 4 g Fibre; 9 g Protein; 250 mg Sodium

Pictured on page 113.

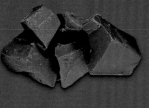

# Macadamia Tortoni

*This decorative dessert will leave your guests in awe of your creative talents! Creamy ice cream and macadamia nuts sit inside a lacy chocolate cup. Delicious!*

### TORTONI

| | | |
|---|---|---|
| Egg white (large), room temperature | 1 | 1 |
| Whipping cream | 1 cup | 250 mL |
| Icing (confectioner's) sugar | 1/3 cup | 75 mL |
| Vanilla | 1 tsp. | 5 mL |
| Finely chopped macadamia nuts, toasted (see Tip, page 20) | 1/3 cup | 75 mL |

### CHOCOLATE CUPS

| | | |
|---|---|---|
| White chocolate melting wafers | 3/4 cup | 175 mL |
| Milk chocolate melting wafers | 3/4 cup | 175 mL |

### GARNISH

Finely chopped macadamia nuts, toasted (see Tip, page 20)

Grated chocolate

Fresh raspberries

**Tortoni:** Beat egg white in small bowl until stiff (not dry) peaks form.

Beat whipping cream, icing sugar and vanilla with same beaters in medium bowl until stiff peaks form. Fold in egg white.

Fold in macadamia nuts. Spread in ungreased 9 inch (22 cm) glass pie plate. Cover tightly with plastic wrap or foil. Freeze for at least 6 hours or overnight until firm.

**Chocolate Cups:** Line inside of six 6 oz. (170 mL) custard cups or shallow fruit nappies with foil. Heat white chocolate in heavy small saucepan on lowest heat, stirring often, until almost melted (see page 17). Do not overheat. Remove from heat. Stir until smooth. Spoon into parchment paper cone (see page 176) or piping bag with small round tip.

Randomly pipe squiggles all over side and bottom of foil, using about 1 tbsp. (15 mL) for each. Chill for about 2 minutes until set.

Repeat with milk chocolate, ensuring that bottom is well coated. It's okay to have spaces showing on sides as it gives a lacy appearance. Chill.

Carefully remove foil and chocolate from custard cups. Gently peel foil from chocolate. Discard foil. Makes 6 cups.

**Garnish:** Just before serving, scoop about four 1 1/2 inch (3.8 cm) balls of Tortoni into each chocolate cup. Divide and sprinkle macadamia nuts over top. Garnish with chocolate and raspberries. Serves 6.

1 serving: 448 Calories; 32.9 g Total Fat (12.9 g Mono, 0.9 g Poly, 17.4 g Sat); 59 mg Cholesterol; 37 g Carbohydrate; 1 g Fibre; 5 g Protein; 63 mg Sodium

Pictured on page 115.

# Frozen Lime Meringue Torte

*This smooth, citrus-flavoured dessert is refreshing and sweet—sure to become a summertime favourite.*

| | | |
|---|---|---|
| Egg whites (large), room temperature | 4 | 4 |
| Granulated sugar | 1 cup | 250 mL |
| **LIME FILLING** | | |
| Can of sweetened condensed milk | 11 oz. | 300 mL |
| Lime juice | 1/2 cup | 125 mL |
| Finely grated lime zest | 1 1/2 tsp. | 7 mL |
| Whipping cream | 2 cups | 500 mL |
| Fresh raspberries | 36 | 36 |
| Lime zest curls, for garnish | | |
| **RASPBERRY SYRUP** | | |
| Package of frozen raspberries in syrup, thawed | 15 oz. | 425 g |

Cut piece of thick cardboard or foam core into 6 × 14 inch (15 × 35 cm) rectangle. Cover with foil (see page 184). Set aside. Line bottom of 11 × 17 inch (28 × 43 cm) baking sheet with parchment (not waxed) paper. Trace two 4 × 12 inch (10 × 30 cm) rectangles, about 2 inches (5 cm) apart, on paper. Turn paper over. Beat egg whites in medium bowl until soft peaks form.

Add sugar, 1 tbsp. (15 mL) at a time, beating well after each addition until sugar is dissolved. Spoon into large piping bag fitted with large open star tip. Pipe to fill each rectangle on paper (see page 15). Bake in 225°F (110°C) oven for about 1 hour until dry. Turn oven off. Let stand in oven, with door slightly ajar, until cooled completely.

**Lime Filling:** Beat condensed milk, lime juice and lime zest in small bowl until smooth and thickened.

Beat whipping cream with same beaters in separate medium bowl until stiff peaks form. Fold in condensed milk mixture. Spoon into large piping bag fitted with large open star tip (see page 175). Secure 1 meringue rectangle to prepared board by piping small line of whipped cream mixture down centre. Gently press meringue rectangle on top. Pipe about 1/2 of remaining whipped cream mixture in thick layer over meringue. Gently press second meringue rectangle on top. Pipe remaining whipped cream mixture on top and around sides.

Arrange raspberries on top. Garnish with lime zest curls. Freeze, uncovered, for at least 6 hours until firm. Cover if storing longer.

**Raspberry Syrup:** Put raspberries and syrup through food mill or sieve into medium saucepan. Discard seeds. Bring syrup to a boil on medium-high. Boil for about 5 minutes until reduced by half and slightly thickened. Cool. Chill until ready to serve. Makes 1 1/4 cups (300 mL) syrup. To serve, cut torte between raspberries into 1 inch (2.5 cm) slices. Cuts into 12 slices. Drizzle about 1 1/2 tbsp. (25 mL) syrup onto each of 12 individual plates. Serves 12.

1 serving: 347 Calories; 16.4 g Total Fat (4.7 g Mono, 0.6 g Poly, 10.2 g Sat); 60 mg Cholesterol; 48 g Carbohydrate; 2 g Fibre; 5 g Protein; 75 mg Sodium

Pictured on page 117.

# Fig 'N' Spice Delight

*The chunky pieces of fruit in the compote go so well with the sweet ice cream. Delicate, wafer-thin tuile baskets hold this tasty treat.*

## HONEY 'N' SPICE ICE CREAM

| | | |
|---|---|---|
| Vanilla ice cream, softened | 6 cups | 1.5 L |
| Liquid honey | 1/2 cup | 125 mL |
| Ground ginger | 1/2 tsp. | 2 mL |
| Ground cinnamon | 1/2 tsp. | 2 mL |
| Ground cloves | 1/8 tsp. | 0.5 mL |

## FIG APRICOT COMPOTE

| | | |
|---|---|---|
| Prepared weak orange pekoe tea | 1 1/2 cups | 375 mL |
| Granulated sugar | 1/3 cup | 75 mL |
| Chopped dried figs | 1/2 cup | 125 mL |
| Chopped dried apricots | 1/4 cup | 60 mL |
| Dried cranberries | 1/4 cup | 60 mL |
| Vanilla | 1/2 tsp. | 2 mL |

## TUILE BASKETS (optional)

| | | |
|---|---|---|
| Egg whites (large), room temperature | 2 | 2 |
| Granulated sugar | 6 tbsp. | 100 mL |
| Almond flavouring | 1/4 tsp. | 1 mL |
| Salt, just a pinch | | |
| Butter (or hard margarine), melted | 1/4 cup | 60 mL |
| All-purpose flour | 1/2 cup | 125 mL |
| Ground ginger | 1/2 tsp. | 2 mL |

Cocoa, for dusting

**Honey 'N' Spice Ice Cream:** Combine all 5 ingredients in large bowl. Spread evenly in ungreased 8 x 8 inch (20 x 20 cm) pan. Cover. Freeze for at least 6 hours or overnight until firm. Makes about 4 cups (1 L) ice cream.

**Fig Apricot Compote:** Heat and stir tea and sugar in medium saucepan on medium-low until sugar is dissolved.

Add next 4 ingredients. Stir. Bring to a boil on medium. Boil gently, uncovered, for about 10 minutes, stirring occasionally, until thickened. Turn into small bowl. Cover. Chill for at least 6 hours, stirring occasionally, until slightly set. Makes 1 1/2 cups (375 mL) compote.

**Tuile Baskets** (see page 178): Line bottom of baking sheet with parchment (not waxed) paper. Trace 2 circles, 6 inches (15 cm) in diameter and about 2 inches (5 cm) apart, on paper. Turn paper over. Whisk first 4 ingredients in medium bowl until frothy and sugar is dissolved.

Whisk in butter. Add flour and ginger. Stir well. Drop 1 1/2 tbsp. (25 mL) batter into each circle. Spread thinly and evenly to fill circles. Bake in 350°F (175°C) oven for about 7 minutes until lightly browned. Working quickly, slide offset spatula under each circle. Place over inverted cups. Using tea towel so you don't burn yourself, carefully press and shape circle onto each cup to form basket. Let stand for about 5 minutes until cool and crisp. Repeat with remaining batter. Makes 10 baskets.

Scoop 1 or 2 ice cream balls into each basket. Divide and spoon compote over ice cream. Sprinkle cocoa on 10 individual plates. Place 1 basket on each plate. Serves 10.

1 serving (without basket): 302 Calories; 9.4 g Total Fat (2.7 g Mono, 0.4 g Poly, 5.7 g Sat); 37 mg Cholesterol; 55 g Carbohydrate; 2 g Fibre; 3 g Protein; 71 mg Sodium

1 basket only: 100 Calories; 5 g Total Fat (1.4 g Mono, 0.2 g Poly, 3.1 g Sat): 13 mg Cholesterol; 13 g Carbohydrate; trace Fibre; 1 g Protein; 61 mg Sodium

Pictured on page 119.

# Pineapple Sorbet

*This creamy, pale yellow sorbet has a cool, tropical flavour. Serve with the golden crisps and fresh pineapple for a special treat.*

| | | |
|---|---|---|
| Granulated sugar | 3/4 cup | 175 mL |
| Water | 1/2 cup | 125 mL |
| Cans of pineapple tidbits (with juice), 14 oz. (398 mL) each | 2 | 2 |
| Lemon juice | 1 tbsp. | 15 mL |
| Egg whites (large), fork-beaten | 2 | 2 |

## MACADAMIA CRISPS

| | | |
|---|---|---|
| Egg whites (large), room temperature | 2 | 2 |
| Granulated sugar | 1/3 cup | 75 mL |
| All-purpose flour | 1/4 cup | 60 mL |
| Ground ginger | 1/4 tsp. | 1 mL |
| Butter (or hard margarine), melted | 1/4 cup | 60 mL |
| Macadamia nuts, toasted (see Tip, page 20) and chopped | 1/3 cup | 75 mL |

Combine sugar and water in medium saucepan. Heat and stir on medium until sugar is dissolved. Bring to a boil. Boil for about 10 minutes, without stirring, until sugar mixture is slightly thickened, but not browned. Cool slightly.

Process pineapple with juice, lemon juice and sugar syrup in blender or food processor until smooth. Pour into ungreased 9 × 13 inch (22 × 33 cm) pan. Freeze, uncovered, for 1 to 2 hours until partially set. Scoop into blender or food processor.

Add egg whites. Process until well combined. Return to same pan. Cover. Freeze for about 3 hours until firm. Makes 6 1/2 cups (1.6 L) sorbet.

**Macadamia Crisps:** Line bottom of 10 × 15 inch (25 × 38 cm) jelly roll pan with parchment (not waxed) paper. Trace 4 circles, 2 3/4 inches (7 cm) in diameter and about 2 to 3 inches (5 to 7.5 cm) apart, on paper. Turn paper over. Beat egg whites in medium bowl until soft peaks form. Gradually add sugar, 1 tbsp. (15 mL) at a time, beating well after each addition until sugar is dissolved.

Fold in next 3 ingredients. Drop 1 tsp. (5 mL) batter into each circle. Spread evenly with offset spatula to fill circles.

Sprinkle each circle with about 1/2 tsp. (2 mL) macadamia nuts. Bake in 350°F (175°C) oven for 5 to 10 minutes until lightly browned. Working quickly, slide offset spatula under each circle. Place on rolling pin to cool completely. Repeat with remaining egg white mixture and macadamia nuts. Makes about 24 crisps. Scoop sorbet into 6 small serving glasses. Serve with Macadamia Crisps. Serves 6.

1 serving (with 4 crisps): 391 Calories; 14.1 g Total Fat (6.9 g Mono, 0.5 g Poly, 6 g Sat); 22 mg Cholesterol; 66 g Carbohydrate; 2 g Fibre; 4 g Protein; 122 mg Sodium

Pictured below.

Top: Pineapple Sorbet, page 118
Bottom: Fig 'N' Spice Delight, page 118

# Cappuccino Soufflés

*This smooth, creamy treat is the perfect ending to any meal. Serve with biscotti.*

| Milk | 1 cup | 250 mL |
| Vanilla | 1 tsp. | 5 mL |
| | | |
| Egg yolks (large) | 2 | 2 |
| Granulated sugar | 1/4 cup | 60 mL |
| | | |
| All-purpose flour | 2 tbsp. | 30 mL |
| Instant coffee granules | 1 tbsp. | 15 mL |
| | | |
| Whipping cream | 1 cup | 250 mL |
| | | |
| Egg whites (large), room temperature | 2 | 2 |
| Cream of tartar | 1/4 tsp. | 1 mL |
| Granulated sugar | 1/3 cup | 75 mL |

Cocoa, sifted if lumpy, for dusting

Cut piece of parchment (or waxed) paper 3 inches (7.5 cm) wide and long enough to go around circumference of 1/3 cup (75 mL) coffee cup or ramekin. Repeat, for a total of 8. If using cups, cut notch for handle. Secure with tape or string, allowing about 1 inch (2.5 cm) above rim of cup. Combine milk and vanilla in medium saucepan. Heat and stir on medium-high until bubbles form around edge of saucepan. Remove from heat.

Whisk egg yolks and first amount of sugar in large bowl until sugar is dissolved.

Whisk in flour and coffee granules. Spoon into milk mixture. Heat and stir on medium for about 5 minutes until thickened. Turn into separate large bowl. Cover. Chill for 1 to 2 hours until cold.

Beat whipping cream in small bowl until soft peaks form. Fold into egg yolk mixture.

Beat egg whites and cream of tartar with clean beaters in separate medium bowl until soft peaks form. Add second amount of sugar, 1 tbsp. (15 mL) at a time, beating well after each addition until sugar is dissolved. Fold into whipped cream mixture. Spoon into prepared cups. Smooth tops. Freeze for at least 6 hours or overnight.

Remove paper. Dust tops of soufflés with cocoa. Serves 8.

1 serving: 197 Calories; 11.7 g Total Fat (3.5 g Mono, 0.5 g Poly, 6.9 g Sat); 92 mg Cholesterol; 20 g Carbohydrate; trace Fibre; 4 g Protein; 44 mg Sodium

Pictured on page 121.

# Peanut Butter Bombes

*Can you imagine anything more delicious than a moist chocolate brownie topped with fudge that oozes out from underneath a creamy peanut butter ice cream? There's one way to find out…*

| Package of brownie mix (reserve icing packet for another use, see Note) | 19 1/2 oz. | 550 g |
| Dry-roasted peanuts, finely chopped | 1/2 cup | 125 mL |
| | | |
| Block of cream cheese, softened | 4 oz. | 125 g |
| Icing (confectioner's) sugar | 1 cup | 250 mL |
| Smooth peanut butter | 1/2 cup | 125 mL |
| Milk | 1/3 cup | 75 mL |
| | | |
| Whipping cream | 1 cup | 250 mL |
| | | |
| Dry-roasted peanuts, finely chopped | 1/4 cup | 60 mL |
| Fudge ice cream topping | 6 tbsp. | 100 mL |

GARNISH
Cocoa
Whipped cream
Chopped dry-roasted peanuts
Grated semi-sweet chocolate

Grease deep 12 inch (30 cm) pizza pan. Line bottom with greased parchment (not waxed) paper (see page 12). Prepare brownie mix according to package directions. Add first amount of peanuts. Stir. Turn into prepared pan. Spread evenly. Bake in 350°F (175°C) oven for about 20 minutes until firm at edge, but still slightly soft in centre. Do not overbake. Let stand in pan on wire rack to cool. Cut out 6 circles, 3 3/4 inches (9.5 cm) in diameter or to fit tops of 3/4 cup (175 mL) custard cups. Remove brownie circles from paper. Set aside. Line six 3/4 cup (175 mL) custard cups or ramekins with plastic wrap large enough to extend over side. Set aside.

Beat next 4 ingredients in medium bowl until smooth.

Beat whipping cream with clean beaters in small bowl until soft peaks form. Fold into cream cheese mixture. Divide among prepared custard cups. Spread evenly.

Divide and sprinkle with second amount of peanuts. Spoon 1 tbsp. (15 mL) fudge topping on each. Place brownie circle on top. Press down gently to meet filling. Cover with plastic wrap. Freeze for at least 8 hours or up to 1 week. Thirty minutes before serving, invert onto individual plates. Remove and discard plastic wrap.

**Garnish:** Dust with cocoa. Add dollop of whipped cream to each plate. Sprinkle with peanuts and chocolate. Serves 6.

1 serving: 1008 Calories; 58.7 g Total Fat (21.8 g Mono, 12.5 g Poly, 21.2 g Sat); 75 mg Cholesterol; 115 g Carbohydrate; 3 g Fibre; 18 g Protein; 497 mg Sodium

Pictured below.

**Note:** Use extra brownie bits and icing packet for trifles, parfaits or sundaes.

Top Left: Peanut Butter Bombes, page 120

Bottom Right: Cappuccino Soufflés, page 120

# Tri-Colour Angel Roll

*This pretty, summery dessert has a light, fruity taste and toasted coconut coating.*

| | | |
|---|---|---|
| Angel food cake mix | 15 oz. | 430 g |
| Lemonade | 1 1/4 cups | 300 mL |
| Finely grated lemon zest | 1 1/2 tsp. | 7 mL |
| Granulated sugar | 1/4 cup | 60 mL |
| Flake coconut, toasted (see Tip, page 20) | 1 cup | 250 mL |
| Raspberry sherbet, softened | 2 cups | 500 mL |
| Lime sherbet, softened | 2 cups | 500 mL |
| Orange sherbet, softened | 2 cups | 500 mL |

Line bottom of ungreased 11 x 17 inch (28 x 43 cm) baking sheet with parchment (or waxed) paper, extending paper 2 inches (5 cm) over long sides (see page 12). Prepare cake mix according to package directions using lemonade instead of water.

Fold in lemon zest. Spread evenly on prepared baking sheet. Bake in 400°F (205°C) oven for about 15 minutes until golden and wooden pick inserted in centre comes out clean.

Spread large tea towel on counter. Cover with piece of parchment (or waxed) paper. Sprinkle sugar and coconut over paper. Invert cake onto sugar mixture. Peel off and discard original parchment paper. Roll up from short end with tea towel. Cool. Unroll cake.

Spoon and spread alternating colours of sherbet, in 1 cup (250 mL) amounts, in 6 rows lengthwise on cake to within 1 inch (2.5 cm) of each edge. Pack down well and smooth together to fill in any spaces. Roll up cake from short end, using towel and paper as guide. Wrap in plastic wrap. Freeze for at least 8 hours or overnight until firm. Trim ends. Cuts into 10 slices.

1 slice: 425 Calories; 8.7 g Total Fat (0.9 g Mono, 0.3 g Poly, 6.9 g Sat); 6 mg Cholesterol; 85 g Carbohydrate; 1 g Fibre; 6 g Protein; 377 mg Sodium

Pictured on page 123.

# Layered Ice Cream Cake

*This colourful dessert is a joy to behold and to eat! Adults and kids will love it.*

| | | |
|---|---|---|
| Vanilla ice cream, softened | 2 1/2 cups | 625 mL |
| Red glazed cherries, chopped | 1/4 cup | 60 mL |
| Chopped glazed pineapple | 1/2 cup | 125 mL |
| Slivered almonds, toasted (see Tip, page 20) | 1/4 cup | 60 mL |
| Semi-sweet chocolate baking squares (1 oz., 28 g, each), grated | 3 | 3 |
| Vanilla ice cream, softened | 3 cups | 750 mL |
| Cocoa, sifted if lumpy | 1/4 cup | 60 mL |
| Whipping cream | 1 1/2 cups | 375 mL |
| Icing (confectioner's) sugar | 1/3 cup | 75 mL |
| Crushed coconut cookies (such as Dad's), about 10 cookies | 1 cup | 250 mL |
| Vanilla | 1 tsp. | 5 mL |
| **GARNISH** | | |
| Chopped red and green glazed cherries | 1/4 cup | 60 mL |
| Chopped glazed pineapple | 2 tbsp. | 30 mL |
| Sliced almonds, toasted (see Tip, page 20) | 2 tbsp. | 30 mL |

Line bottom and side of 8 inch (20 cm) springform pan with parchment (or waxed) paper (see page 12). Combine first 4 ingredients in large bowl. Spread evenly in prepared pan. Freeze for 1 to 2 hours until almost firm.

Combine next 3 ingredients in same large bowl. Spread evenly over ice cream mixture. Freeze for 2 to 3 hours until almost firm.

Beat whipping cream in small bowl until soft peaks form. Add icing sugar. Beat well.

Add cookies and vanilla. Mix well. Spread evenly over chocolate mixture. Freeze for at least 8 hours or overnight until firm.

**Garnish:** Sprinkle top with cherries, pineapple and almonds. Cut with hot knife. Serves 10 to 12.

1 serving: 497 Calories; 28.3 g Total Fat (8.2 g Mono, 1.2 g Poly, 17.3 g Sat); 78 mg Cholesterol; 60 g Carbohydrate; 1 g Fibre; 6 g Protein; 137 mg Sodium

Pictured on page 123.

Top: Layered Ice Cream Cake, above
Bottom: Tri-Colour Angel Roll, this page

# Meringues

Light, airy and wonderfully versatile,
these delicate desserts are so easy to make! After a
savoury meal, a fruity meringue stack or a layered meringue
cake is just the thing to satisfy your sweet tooth.

# Chocolate Hazelnut Desserts

*A rich, melt-in-your-mouth filling
is sandwiched between two crisp meringues
and drizzled with a warm chocolate sauce. This
dessert's flavours go very well with coffee.*

| CHOCOLATE MERINGUES | | |
| --- | --- | --- |
| Egg whites (large), room temperature | 4 | 4 |
| Cream of tartar | 1/2 tsp. | 2 mL |
| Granulated sugar | 1 cup | 250 mL |
| Cocoa, sifted if lumpy | 3 tbsp. | 50 mL |
| **HAZELNUT FILLING** | | |
| Block of cream cheese, softened | 4 oz. | 125 g |
| Icing (confectioner's) sugar | 2 tbsp. | 30 mL |
| Hazelnut-flavoured liqueur (such as Frangelico) | 1 1/2 tbsp. | 25 mL |
| Chocolate hazelnut spread (such as Nutella) | 1/2 cup | 125 mL |
| **CHOCOLATE SAUCE** | | |
| Semi-sweet chocolate baking squares (1 oz., 28 g, each), chopped | 6 | 6 |
| Half-and-half cream | 1/3 cup | 75 mL |

**Chocolate Meringues:** Grease 2 baking sheets. Line bottom with parchment (not waxed) paper. Beat egg whites and cream of tartar in large bowl until soft peaks form.

Add sugar, 1 tbsp. (15 mL) at a time, beating until sugar is dissolved.

Fold in cocoa. Spoon into piping bag fitted with large plain tip. Pipe 36 circles, about 1 1/2 inches (3.8 cm) in diameter and 1 1/2 inches (3.8 cm) apart, on paper (see page 15). Bake in 225°F (110°C) oven for about 1 1/4 hours until dry. Turn oven off. Let stand in oven with door slightly ajar until cool. Makes 36 meringues.

**Hazelnut Filling:** Beat all 4 ingredients in separate large bowl until well combined. Makes about 1 cup (250 mL) filling. Spread 1 tbsp. (15 mL) filling onto 1 meringue. Top with another meringue. Repeat with remaining meringues and filling, to make 6 desserts.

**Chocolate Sauce:** Heat chocolate and cream in small heavy saucepan on lowest heat, stirring often, until chocolate is almost melted (see page 17). Do not overheat. Remove from heat. Stir until smooth. Makes 1 cup (250 mL) sauce. Place 3 sandwiched meringues on each of 6 individual plates. Drizzle with chocolate sauce. Serves 6.

1 serving: 535 Calories; 29 g Total Fat (10.9 g Mono, 3.8 g Poly, 13 g Sat); 27 mg Cholesterol; 64 g Carbohydrate; 4 g Fibre; 12 g Protein; 214 mg Sodium

Pictured below.

# Masala Meringue Kisses

*Mah-SAH-lah is a word used in India to describe a variety of spice blends. The unique combination of spices in this meringue is wonderfully exotic.*

| | | |
|---|---|---|
| Granulated sugar | 3/4 cup | 175 mL |
| Ground cinnamon | 1/2 tsp. | 2 mL |
| Ground cardamom | 1/2 tsp. | 2 mL |
| Ground ginger | 1/4 tsp. | 1 mL |
| White (or black) pepper | 1/8 tsp. | 0.5 mL |
| Egg whites (large), room temperature | 3 | 3 |
| Cream of tartar | 1/2 tsp. | 2 mL |
| Milk chocolate chips | 1/4 cup | 60 mL |
| Butterscotch chips | 1/4 cup | 60 mL |
| BRITTLE CREAM | | |
| Whipping cream | 1 cup | 250 mL |
| Vanilla | 1 tsp. | 5 mL |
| Broken peanut brittle | 1/3 cup | 75 mL |

Line bottoms of 2 baking sheets with parchment (not waxed) paper. On 1 paper, trace 4 circles, 4 inches (10 cm) in diameter and about 1 1/2 inches (3.8 cm) apart. Turn paper over. Combine first 5 ingredients in small bowl.

Beat egg whites and cream of tartar in medium bowl until soft peaks form. Add sugar mixture, 1 tbsp. (15 mL) at a time, beating well after each addition until sugar is dissolved. Spoon into piping bag fitted with large plain tip. Pipe onto circles, filling in each circle completely (see page 15). Pipe remaining mixture into kisses by holding bag straight up over desired piping area on second baking sheet. Gently squeeze bag for about 2 seconds until small amount comes out. Quickly lift bag to form small peak. Bake in 225°F (110°C) oven for about 45 minutes until dry. Turn oven off. Let stand in oven with door slightly ajar until cool. Makes 4 meringues and 16 to 20 kisses.

Heat chocolate and butterscotch chips in separate small heavy saucepans on lowest heat, stirring often, until almost melted. Do not overheat. Remove from heat. Stir until smooth. Dip 1/2 of each kiss into chocolate and 1/2 into butterscotch. Let stand until set.

**Brittle Cream:** Beat whipping cream and vanilla in separate small bowl until stiff peaks form.

Process peanut brittle in blender or food processor until ground. Fold into whipped cream mixture. Makes about 2 cups (500 mL) cream. Place 1 meringue circle on each of 4 individual plates. Spoon about 1/2 cup (125 mL) cream onto each meringue. Top with dipped kisses, pressing down slightly to push cream to edges. Serves 4.

1 serving: 516 Calories; 26.5 g Total Fat (8.2 g Mono, 1.3 g Poly, 15.5 g Sat); 78 mg Cholesterol; 67 g Carbohydrate; trace Fibre; 6 g Protein; 136 mg Sodium

Pictured on page 127.

## About Meringues

*Meringues can be used as topping for pies and other desserts, baked into cookies, incorporated into other mixtures, or piped onto desserts for decorative look.*

Some secrets to making the perfect meringue are:

- Carefully separate egg whites and egg yolks when cold, but let egg whites warm to room temperature before beating. Fat reduces volume of whipped egg whites, so make sure there is no trace of egg yolk remaining in egg whites. Make sure all beaters, bowls and spatulas are free of grease. Don't whip in plastic or wooden containers because they retain grease even when washed. Aluminum bowls will react with egg whites, turning them a greyish colour. Beating in copper bowl will create fluffier egg whites. If you do not have a copper bowl, use a stainless steel, glass or ceramic bowl.

- Don't underbeat or overbeat egg whites.

- Once whipping egg whites has begun, don't stop partway through process. They will deflate if left to sit for more than 5 minutes.

- Begin beating egg whites slowly and increase speed gradually when they become frothy. Add sugar, about 1 tbsp. (15 mL) at a time, and beat until dissolved.

- Chill custard and cream meringue-topped pies because of food safety issues. All other meringue desserts should be stored at room temperature in airtight containers.

- For meringue-topped pies, spread meringue over hot filling and make sure it extends to, and touches, crust. This will prevent meringue from shrinking and pulling away from sides of pie or tart.

# Almond Peach Meringue Nests

*A crisp, light meringue shell filled with a creamy, caramel-nut mixture. The flavour of the peach schnapps is evident in the aftertaste.*

| | | |
|---|---|---|
| Egg whites (large), room temperature | 4 | 4 |
| Cream of tartar | 1 tsp. | 5 mL |
| Granulated sugar | 2/3 cup | 150 mL |
| Icing (confectioner's) sugar | 2/3 cup | 150 mL |
| **ALMOND PEACH FILLING** | | |
| Whole blanched almonds | 1/2 cup | 125 mL |
| Granulated sugar | 1/2 cup | 125 mL |
| Water | 1/4 cup | 60 mL |
| Mascarpone cheese | 8 oz. | 250 g |
| Peach schnapps | 2 tbsp. | 30 mL |
| Liquid honey | 2 tbsp. | 30 mL |
| Can of sliced peaches, drained | 14 oz. | 398 mL |

Line bottoms of 2 baking sheets with parchment (not waxed) paper. Trace 4 circles, 3 inches (7.5 cm) in diameter and about 1 1/2 inches (3.8 cm) apart, on each paper. Turn paper over. Beat egg whites and cream of tartar in large bowl until soft peaks form.

Add granulated sugar, 1 tbsp. (15 mL) at a time, beating well after each addition until sugar is dissolved.

Fold in icing sugar. Reserve 1/2. Divide and spoon remaining egg white mixture onto circles. Spread evenly. Spoon reserved egg white mixture into piping bag fitted with small open star tip. Create nest by piping remaining meringue around edge of each circle twice. Bake in 225°F (110°C) oven for about 1 hour until dry. Turn oven off. Let stand in oven with door slightly ajar until cool. Makes 8 nests.

**Almond Peach Filling:** Arrange almonds close together in single layer on greased baking sheet.

Combine sugar and water in medium saucepan. Heat and stir on medium-low until sugar is dissolved. Bring to a boil on medium-high. Boil, uncovered, for about 8 minutes, without stirring, until deep golden brown. Drizzle over almonds. Let stand for about 20 minutes until set. Break into pieces. Process in blender or food processor until coarsely chopped. Transfer to medium bowl.

Add next 3 ingredients. Stir. Makes 1 1/2 cups (375 mL) filling. Spoon 3 tbsp. (50 mL) filling into each nest.

Arrange 2 to 3 peach slices on top of filling. Serves 8.

1 serving: 368 Calories; 15.8 g Total Fat (6.3 g Mono, 1.4 g Poly, 7.3 g Sat); 34 mg Cholesterol; 52 g Carbohydrate; 1 g Fibre; 6 g Protein; 123 mg Sodium

Pictured on page 129.

# Lemon Curd Meringue Stacks

*These elegant desserts look summery. Layers of tart Lemon Curd are alternated with layers of sweet meringue. Make the Lemon Curd up to one week ahead and store in the refrigerator.*

| | | |
|---|---|---|
| **LEMON CURD** | | |
| Large eggs | 3 | 3 |
| Granulated sugar | 1/3 cup | 75 mL |
| Lemon juice | 1/2 cup | 125 mL |
| Butter (not margarine), cut up | 1/2 cup | 125 mL |
| Finely grated lemon zest | 2 tsp. | 10 mL |
| **MERINGUE CIRCLES** | | |
| Egg whites (large), room temperature | 4 | 4 |
| Cream of tartar | 1 tsp. | 5 mL |
| Granulated sugar | 1 cup | 250 mL |
| **RASPBERRY SAUCE** | | |
| Whole frozen raspberries, thawed (with juice) | 3 cups | 750 mL |
| Granulated sugar | 1/4 cup | 60 mL |
| Raspberry (or regular) vodka | 1 1/2 tbsp. | 25 mL |
| Whole fresh raspberries, for garnish | | |
| Fresh mint leaves, for garnish | | |

**Lemon Curd:** Whisk eggs and sugar in medium saucepan until frothy and sugar is dissolved.

Add lemon juice. Heat and whisk on medium for about 2 minutes until warm.

Add butter, 1/4 at a time, whisking constantly, until butter is melted and mixture is thickened.

Add lemon zest. Stir. Makes 1 3/4 cups (425 mL) curd. Turn into medium bowl. Cover. Chill for at least 6 hours or overnight, stirring occasionally, until thickened.

**Meringue Circles:** Line bottoms of 2 baking sheets with parchment (not waxed) paper. Trace 6 circles, 3 1/2 inches (9 cm) in diameter and about 1 1/2 inches (3.8 cm) apart, on each paper. Turn paper over. Beat egg whites and cream of tartar in separate medium bowl until soft peaks form.

Add sugar, 1 tbsp. (15 mL) at a time, beating well after each addition until sugar is dissolved. Spoon into piping bag fitted with large plain tip. Pipe onto circles, filling in each circle completely (see page 15). Bake in 225°F (110°C) oven for about 45 minutes until dry. Turn oven off. Let stand in oven with door slightly ajar until cool. Makes 12 meringues. Spread 2 tbsp. (30 mL) curd on each of 4 meringues. Carefully stack to make 4. Spread 2 tbsp. (30 mL) curd on top. Top with remaining meringues. Cover. Chill for 1 to 3 hours until meringues are softened.

**Raspberry Sauce:** Combine frozen raspberries with juice, sugar and vodka in small saucepan. Heat and stir on medium-low until sugar is dissolved. Simmer, uncovered, for about 5 minutes, without stirring, until slightly thickened. Press raspberry mixture through sieve into small bowl. Discard solids. Stir. Makes 1 cup (250 mL) sauce. Divide and drizzle sauce on 4 individual plates (see pages 182 and 183). Top with meringue stacks.

Garnish individual servings with fresh raspberries and mint leaves. Serves 4.

1 serving: 838 Calories; 28.4 g Total Fat (8.5 g Mono, 1.6 g Poly, 16.3 g Sat); 227 mg Cholesterol; 140 g Carbohydrate; 9 g Fibre; 10 g Protein; 353 mg Sodium

Pictured below.

Top Left: Lemon Curd Meringue Stacks, page 128

Bottom Right: Almond Peach Meringue Nests, page 128

# Mango Torte

*You'll be able to close your eyes and imagine that you are in the tropics when you taste this refreshing dessert.*

| | | |
|---|---|---|
| Egg whites (large), room temperature | 4 | 4 |
| Cream of tartar | 1/2 tsp. | 2 mL |
| Granulated sugar | 1 cup | 250 mL |
| Macadamia nuts, toasted (see Tip, page 20) and finely chopped | 2/3 cup | 150 mL |
| Can of sliced mango, drained | 14 oz. | 398 mL |
| Whipping cream | 1 1/2 cups | 375 mL |
| Icing (confectioner's) sugar | 1/2 cup | 125 mL |
| Passion fruit pulp (about 4 – 6 passion fruit) | 1/2 cup | 125 mL |
| Granulated sugar | 1/3 cup | 75 mL |
| Can of sliced mango, drained and cut into thin slices | 14 oz. | 398 mL |

Line bottoms of 2 baking sheets with parchment (not waxed) paper. Trace 3 circles, 7 inches (18 cm) in diameter and about 2 inches (5 cm) apart, in total. Turn paper over. Beat egg whites and cream of tartar in large bowl until soft peaks form.

Add sugar, 1 tbsp. (15 mL) at a time, until sugar is dissolved.

Fold in macadamia nuts. Divide and spoon onto circles. Spread evenly. Bake in 325°F (160°C) oven for about 50 minutes until golden and dry. Let stand on baking sheets until cool.

Purée mango in blender or food processor.

Beat whipping cream in medium bowl until soft peaks form. Beat in icing sugar until well combined. Add puréed mango. Stir. Place 1 meringue on serving plate. Spread 1/3 of filling on top. Top with second meringue. Spread with 1/2 of remaining filling. Top with third meringue. Spread remaining filling on top. Cover. Chill for at least 8 hours or overnight.

Combine passion fruit pulp and sugar in frying pan. Heat and stir on medium for about 5 minutes until slightly thickened. Cool. Strain syrup, reserving 2 tbsp. (30 mL) seeds. Stir reserved seeds back into syrup. Discard any remaining seeds.

Arrange mango slices on top of torte. Drizzle syrup over top. Serve immediately. Cuts into 8 wedges.

1 wedge: 445 Calories; 24.1 g Total Fat (11.4 g Mono, 0.6 g Poly, 10.8 g Sat); 55 mg Cholesterol; 57 g Carbohydrate; 4 g Fibre; 4 g Protein; 49 mg Sodium

Pictured on page 130/131.

*Meringues*

# Hazelnut Meringue Torte

*This delectable torte combines a variety of irresistible flavours and textures. Layers of sweet cream, chocolate and meringue are coated in a crunchy praline.*

| | | |
|---|---|---|
| Whole hazelnuts (filberts), toasted (see Tip, page 20) and skins removed (see page 17) | 1 cup | 250 mL |
| Egg whites (large), room temperature | 4 | 4 |
| Cream of tartar | 1 tsp. | 5 mL |
| Granulated sugar | 1 cup | 250 mL |
| **BROWN SUGAR CREAM FILLING** | | |
| Whipping cream | 1 1/2 cups | 375 mL |
| Brown sugar, packed | 3 tbsp. | 50 mL |
| Coffee-flavoured liqueur (such as Kahlúa) | 2 tbsp. | 30 mL |
| Semi-sweet chocolate baking squares (1 oz., 28 g, each), chopped | 4 | 4 |
| **HAZELNUT PRALINE** | | |
| Hazelnuts (filberts), toasted (see Tip, page 20) and skins removed (see page 17) | 3/4 cup | 175 mL |
| Granulated sugar | 1 1/4 cups | 300 mL |
| Water | 1/2 cup | 125 mL |
| **GARNISH** | | |
| Semi-sweet chocolate baking squares (1 oz., 28 g, each) | 3 | 3 |
| Whole hazelnuts (filberts), toasted (see Tip, page 20) | 15 | 15 |

Process hazelnuts in blender or food processor until finely chopped or resembles fine crumbs.

Line bottoms of 2 baking sheets with parchment (not waxed) paper. Trace two 4 x 8 inch (10 x 20 cm) rectangles on each paper. Turn paper over. Beat egg whites and cream of tartar in large bowl until soft peaks form.

Add sugar, 1 tbsp. (15 mL) at a time, until sugar is dissolved. Fold in hazelnuts.

Divide and spoon onto rectangles. Spread evenly. Bake in 325°F (160°C) oven for 30 minutes until lightly browned and dry. Let stand on baking sheets until cool.

**Brown Sugar Cream Filling:** Beat whipping cream and brown sugar in medium bowl until soft peaks form.

Stir in liqueur. Makes 3 cups (750 mL) filling. Reserve 1/2 of filling.

Heat chocolate in small heavy saucepan on lowest heat for about 3 minutes, stirring often, until almost melted. Do not overheat. Remove from heat. Stir until smooth.

Place 1 meringue rectangle on long 10 inch (25 cm) serving plate or cake board (see page 184). Spread 1/3 of chocolate on top. Spread 1/3 of remaining filling over chocolate. Top with second meringue rectangle. Spread with 1/2 of remaining of chocolate, then 1/2 of remaining filling. Top with third meringue rectangle. Repeat layers with remaining chocolate and filling. Top with fourth meringue rectangle. Spread top and sides with reserved filling. Chill for 8 hours or overnight.

**Hazelnut Praline** (see page 16): Spread hazelnuts in single layer, touching, on lightly greased baking sheet.

Combine sugar and water in medium saucepan. Heat and stir on medium-low until sugar is dissolved. Bring to a boil on medium-high. Boil, uncovered, for 5 to 10 minutes, without stirring, until deep golden brown. Drizzle over nuts. Let stand for 20 minutes until hard. Break into pieces. Process in food processor until coarsely chopped or put into plastic bag and crush with mallet or rolling pin. Makes 3 1/2 cups (875 mL) praline. Press praline into bottom and sides of torte.

**Garnish:** Heat chocolate in small heavy saucepan on lowest heat until almost melted (see page 17). Do not overheat. Remove from heat. Stir until smooth. Dip tips of whole hazelnuts into chocolate. Place on waxed paper until dry. Drizzle remaining chocolate over torte. Sprinkle remaining praline over top. Arrange hazelnuts on top. Cut with serrated knife into 8 slices. Serves 8.

1 serving: 669 Calories; 37.7 g Total Fat (20.2 g Mono, 2.4 g Poly, 13.3 g Sat); 55 mg Cholesterol; 82 g Carbohydrate; 3 g Fibre; 7 g Protein; 50 mg Sodium

Pictured below.

# Pastries & Tarts

Begin your adventure into this section by creating a
classic pie with a decadent twist. Then take a bold leap into
the world of strudels, tarts, flans and individual-sized pastries.
You'll never tire of experimenting with these delightful delicacies.

# Apple Strudel

*An appealing golden roll filled with a sweet apple cinnamon filling. Drizzle with warm maple syrup, and serve with a scoop of ice cream and Tuile Cutout, page 179.*

|  | | |
|---|---|---|
| Tart medium cooking apples (such as Granny Smith), peeled and sliced | 5 | 5 |
| Brown sugar, packed | 3/4 cup | 175 mL |
| Fine dry bread crumbs | 1/2 cup | 125 mL |
| Ground cinnamon | 1 tsp. | 5 mL |
| Finely grated orange zest | 3/4 tsp. | 4 mL |
| Ground ginger | 1/2 tsp. | 2 mL |
| Phyllo pastry sheets | 6 | 6 |
| Butter (or hard margarine), melted | 1/3 cup | 75 mL |
| Granulated sugar | 1 1/2 tbsp. | 25 mL |

Combine first 6 ingredients in large bowl.

Lay tea towel on work surface, short end closest to you. Place 1 pastry sheet on towel, lining up short end of sheet with closest towel end. Place second pastry sheet at far end of first sheet with 6 inches (15 cm) overlapping in middle. Working quickly, brush pastry (now 1 long sheet) with butter. Layer 2 pastry sheets over butter in same manner as before. Brush with butter. Repeat with remaining pastry sheets and some butter, keeping covered with damp tea towel.

Mound apple mixture onto pastry, 6 inches (15 cm) from closest edge. Fold closest edge of pastry up and over apple mixture. Roll up tightly to enclose filling, using tea towel as guide. Pack any loose apple mixture back into roll. Leave ends open. Place on greased baking sheet. Brush roll with remaining butter. Sprinkle with granulated sugar. Bake in 350°F (175°C) oven for about 55 minutes until golden brown and crisp. Let stand for 10 minutes. Cuts into six 2 inch (5 cm) slices.

1 slice: 375 Calories; 12.8 g Total Fat (3.6 g Mono, 1.3 g Poly, 7.1 g Sat); 29 mg Cholesterol; 65 g Carbohydrate; 3 g Fibre; 3 g Protein; 296 mg Sodium

Pictured below.

# Cream Cheese Strudels

*Golden, flaky pastries with a delicious berry and cream cheese filling. A wonderful balance of flavours.*

**FILLING**

| | | |
|---|---|---|
| All-purpose flour | 2 tbsp. | 30 mL |
| Granulated sugar | 2 tbsp. | 30 mL |
| Block of cream cheese, softened | 4 oz. | 125 g |
| Lemon juice | 1 tsp. | 5 mL |
| Package of frozen puff pastry, thawed according to package directions | 14 oz. | 397 g |
| Mixed berry spread (or jam) | 1/4 cup | 60 mL |
| Large egg, fork-beaten | 1 | 1 |
| Sanding (decorating) sugar (see Note) or granulated sugar | 1 tbsp. | 15 mL |

**Filling:** Combine flour and granulated sugar in small cup.

Beat cream cheese and lemon juice in small bowl until smooth. Add flour mixture. Beat well. Chill for 1 hour. Makes 2/3 cup (150 mL) filling.

Roll out 1/2 of pastry on lightly floured surface to 6 × 12 inch (15 × 30 cm) rectangle.

Spread pastry with 2 tbsp. (30 mL) berry spread, leaving 1 inch (2.5 cm) border on short ends and on long side farthest from you.

Spoon 1/2 of filling, in dabs, over berry spread along closest long side.

Brush exposed pastry with egg.

Roll up, jelly roll-style, starting with closest long side. Pinch side edges together to seal. Place, seam-side down, on lightly greased or parchment (not waxed) paper-lined baking sheet. Brush roll with egg.

Using sharp knife, cut slits across top at 1 1/2 inch (3.8 cm) intervals, down to filling layer. Sprinkle roll with 1 1/2 tsp. (7 mL) sanding sugar. Repeat with remaining pastry, berry spread, filling and sanding sugar. Bake in 400°F (205°C) oven for about 25 minutes until puffed and golden. Remove to wire rack to cool. Cut each roll into 3 slices. Serves 6.

1 serving: 527 Calories; 33.4 g Total Fat (8.2 g Mono, 14.9 g Poly, 8.4 g Sat); 59 mg Cholesterol; 50 g Carbohydrate; trace Fibre; 8 g Protein; 243 mg Sodium

Pictured on page 137.

**Note:** Sanding sugar is a coarse decorating sugar that resembles the coloured sugar frequently used at Christmastime. It gives a special look to fancy desserts and pastries. Available in specialty kitchen stores.

Are there a few pastry scraps left over? Roll them out, sprinkle with cinnamon and sugar, and bake like cookies. Yum!

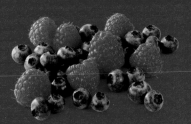

# Poppy Seed 'N' Orange Pastries

*These miniature cream puffs, called profiteroles (pruh-FIHT-uh-rohls), have a sweet orange filling. An elegant dessert with a fresh citrus flavour.*

## ORANGE CURD

| | | |
|---|---|---|
| Large eggs | 4 | 4 |
| Granulated sugar | 2/3 cup | 150 mL |
| Lemon juice | 1/3 cup | 75 mL |
| Orange juice | 1/4 cup | 60 mL |
| Butter (not margarine) | 2/3 cup | 150 mL |
| Finely grated orange zest | 1 1/2 tbsp. | 25 mL |

## POPPY SEED PROFITEROLES

| | | |
|---|---|---|
| Water | 1 cup | 250 mL |
| Butter (or hard margarine) | 6 tbsp. | 100 mL |
| All-purpose flour | 1 1/4 cups | 300 mL |
| Salt, just a pinch | | |
| Large eggs | 4 | 4 |
| Poppy seeds | 1 – 2 tsp. | 5 – 10 mL |

## ORANGE LIQUEUR SYRUP

| | | |
|---|---|---|
| Orange juice | 1/2 cup | 125 mL |
| Granulated sugar | 1/2 cup | 125 mL |
| Orange-flavoured liqueur (such as Grand Marnier) | 1/4 cup | 60 mL |

**Orange Curd:** Whisk eggs and sugar in large saucepan until well combined.

Add lemon juice, orange juice and butter. Heat and stir on medium for about 10 minutes until butter is melted and mixture is thickened. Remove from heat.

Add orange zest. Stir. Turn into medium bowl. Cool. Cover. Chill for at least 8 hours or overnight. Makes 2 1/4 cups (550 mL) orange curd.

**Poppy Seed Profiteroles:** Heat water and butter in medium saucepan on medium-high, stirring constantly, until butter is melted. Bring to a boil.

Add flour and salt. Stir vigorously for about 1 minute until mixture pulls away from side of saucepan to form soft dough. Transfer to large bowl.

Add 1 egg.

Beat well until dough is thick and glossy. Repeat with remaining eggs, 1 at a time, beating well after each addition.

Spoon dough into piping bag fitted with large closed star tip. Sprinkle drops of water onto 2 ungreased baking sheets to create steam that helps pastries rise and be fluffy. Pipe 18 rosettes (see page 15), about 2 inches (5 cm) apart, onto baking sheets. Sprinkle with poppy seeds. Bake in 425°F (220°C) oven for about 30 minutes until puffed and golden. Remove pastries to wire racks to cool. Return to baking sheets. Cut tops off pastries and reserve.

Scoop out soft dough from inside and discard. Spoon 2 tbsp. (30 mL) orange curd into each pastry. Replace tops.

**Orange Liqueur Syrup:** Heat orange juice, sugar and liqueur in small frying pan on medium, stirring constantly, until sugar is dissolved. Bring to a boil on medium-high. Boil for 5 to 10 minutes until thickened. Makes 1/2 cup (125 mL) syrup. Drizzle some syrup onto each of 6 individual plates (see page 183). Divide profiteroles among plates. Drizzle remaining syrup on top. Serves 6.

1 serving: 697 Calories; 40.4 g Total Fat (12.2 g Mono, 2.4 g Poly, 22.8 g Sat); 377 mg Cholesterol; 68 g Carbohydrate; 1 g Fibre; 12 g Protein; 423 mg Sodium

Pictured below.

# Raspberry Pastries

*Crisp, golden pastry nests topped with a fluffy
ricotta cheese mixture and a sweet, red glaze.
The contrasting flavours and textures are delightful.*

| RICOTTA TOPPING | | |
|---|---|---|
| Ricotta cheese | 1 cup | 250 mL |
| Raspberry jam | 3 tbsp. | 50 mL |
| Orange-flavoured liqueur (such as Grand Marnier) | 1 tbsp. | 15 mL |
| Vanilla | 1/4 tsp. | 1 mL |
| Whipping cream | 1/2 cup | 125 mL |
| Icing (confectioner's) sugar | 3 tbsp. | 50 mL |
| Bittersweet chocolate baking square, finely grated (chilled before and after grating) | 1 oz. | 28 g |
| Phyllo pastry sheets | 8 | 8 |
| Butter (or hard margarine), melted | 1/3 cup | 75 mL |

| JELLY GLAZE | | |
|---|---|---|
| Raspberry jelly (or sieved raspberry jam) | 1/3 cup | 75 mL |
| Water | 3 tbsp. | 50 mL |
| White corn syrup | 2 tbsp. | 30 mL |

| GARNISH | | |
|---|---|---|
| Melted chocolate | | |
| Whipped cream | 1 cup | 250 mL |
| Shaved chocolate (or chocolate curls) | | |
| Fresh raspberries | | |

**Ricotta Topping:** Beat first 4 ingredients in medium bowl for about 5 minutes until fluffy and slightly thickened.

Beat whipping cream and icing sugar with clean beaters in small bowl until stiff peaks form. Add to cheese mixture. Add grated chocolate. Fold in. Cover. Chill for up to 8 hours. Makes 2 cups (500 mL) topping.

Place 1 pastry sheet on work surface with long side closest to you. Brush top half with butter. Fold bottom half over top half. Brush with butter. Roll up, jelly roll-style, from long side.

Twist several times, while coiling loosely, into 3 1/2 inch (9 cm) circle. Tuck end underneath to hold nest-like shape. Place on ungreased baking sheet. Repeat with remaining pastry sheets and butter. Lightly brush any remaining butter on top of pastries. Bake in 350°F (175°C) oven for 18 to 20 minutes until golden brown.

**Jelly Glaze:** Heat jelly, water and corn syrup in small saucepan on medium for about 6 minutes, stirring often, until boiling and syrupy. Makes about 1/2 cup (125 mL) glaze. Spoon about 1 tbsp. (15 mL) hot glaze over each pastry. Let stand for 1 hour. Cover. Store at room temperature for up to 3 days.

Just before serving, drizzle melted chocolate onto individual plates (see page 183). Place 1 pastry on each plate. Spoon about 1/4 cup (60 mL) Ricotta Topping on each pastry. Garnish with whipped cream, shaved chocolate (see page 177) and raspberries. Serves 8.

1 serving: 381 Calories; 24.6 g Total Fat (7.1 g Mono, 1.4 g Poly, 14.8 g Sat); 75 mg Cholesterol; 35 g Carbohydrate; trace Fibre; 6 g Protein; 225 mg Sodium

Pictured on page 141.

# Strawberry Cream Layers

*Layers of golden pastry alternate with a fluffy, pink filling.
Garnish with a strawberry half for a special touch.*

| | | |
|---|---|---|
| Package of frozen puff pastry (14 oz., 397 g, size), thawed according to package directions | 1/2 | 1/2 |

| STRAWBERRY FILLING | | |
|---|---|---|
| Chopped fresh strawberries | 1 1/2 cups | 375 mL |
| Strawberry jam, warmed | 1/3 cup | 75 mL |
| Icing (confectioner's) sugar | 1/4 cup | 60 mL |
| Orange-flavoured liqueur (such as Grand Marnier) | 1 – 2 tbsp. | 15 – 30 mL |
| Whipping cream | 1 cup | 250 mL |

| GARNISH | | |
|---|---|---|
| Icing (confectioner's) sugar | | |
| Pink chocolate melting wafers, melted | | |
| Chocolate melting wafers, melted | | |

Roll out pastry on lightly floured surface to 12 inch (30 cm) square. Place on greased baking sheet. Grease bottom of another baking sheet. Place directly on top of pastry. Bake in 450°F (230°C) oven for 15 to 20 minutes until golden brown. Remove to wire rack to cool. Cut into 12 rectangles.

**Strawberry Filling:** Combine first 4 ingredients in large bowl. Cover. Chill for 30 minutes. Drain, reserving syrup.

Beat whipping cream in small bowl until soft peaks form. Fold in strawberry mixture. Makes about 3 cups (750 mL) filling. Place 1 pastry rectangle on baking sheet. Top with 6 tbsp. (100 mL) filling. Place another pastry rectangle over filling. Top with 6 tbsp. (100 mL) filling. Top with third pastry rectangle over filling. Repeat with remaining pastry and filling to make total of 4 individual desserts.

Sprinkle tops liberally with icing sugar to cover. Drizzle chocolate or reserved syrup onto 4 individual plates (see page 183). Carefully place 1 dessert on each plate. Serves 4.

1 serving: 591 Calories; 39.4 g Total Fat (10.3 g Mono, 11.6 g Poly, 15.3 g Sat); 73 mg Cholesterol; 55 g Carbohydrate; 2 g Fibre; 6 g Protein; 158 mg Sodium

Pictured below.

Top: Strawberry Cream Layers, page 140
Bottom: Raspberry Pastries, page 140

# Caramel Apple Pie

*A tart apple pie with a beautifully glazed lattice top. The addition of caramel adds a decadent sweetness to the pie.*

| | | |
|---|---|---|
| Pastry for 2 crust pie, your own or a mix | | |
| Caramel ice cream topping | 3/4 cup | 175 mL |
| Block of cream cheese, softened | 8 oz. | 250 g |
| Large egg | 1 | 1 |
| Lemon juice | 1 tbsp. | 15 mL |
| Ground cinnamon | 1/2 tsp. | 2 mL |
| Tart medium cooking apples (such as Granny Smith), peeled and thinly sliced | 5 | 5 |
| Pecans, toasted (see Tip, page 20) and finely chopped | 1 1/2 cups | 375 mL |
| Brown sugar, packed | 1/4 cup | 60 mL |
| Egg yolk (large), fork-beaten | 1 | 1 |

Roll out large 1/2 of pastry on lightly floured surface to fit ungreased 9 inch (22 cm) pie plate. Carefully lift pastry (see page 14) and press into bottom and up side of pie plate, leaving 1/2 inch (12 mm) overhang.

Beat next 5 ingredients in large bowl until smooth.

Add apple. Stir until coated. Sprinkle bottom of pie shell with pecans. Turn apple mixture into pie shell. Sprinkle with brown sugar.

Roll out second 1/2 of pastry on lightly floured surface to 9 x 11 inch (22 x 28 cm) rectangle. Cut into eleven 3/4 inch (2 cm) strips with fluted pastry cutter. Dampen both ends of strips with water.

Place strips 1/2 inch (12 mm) apart across apple mixture. Gently press dampened ends of strips against pastry edge to secure. Brush strips with egg yolk. Repeat with remaining strips in opposite direction.

Trim and crimp edge to seal. Brush strips with egg yolk. Bake on bottom rack in 450°F (230°C) oven for 10 minutes. Reduce heat to 350°F (175°C). Bake for 45 to 50 minutes until apple is tender and crust is golden. Serve warm. Cuts into 8 wedges.

1 wedge: 599 Calories; 38.5 g Total Fat (18.3 g Mono, 5.8 g Poly, 11.9 g Sat); 88 mg Cholesterol; 62 g Carbohydrate; 3 g Fibre; 7 g Protein; 422 mg Sodium

Pictured on page 143.

# Orange Sabayon Blueberry Pie

*Sabayon (pronounced sah-bah-YAWN) is the French word for the warm orange froth that is served over this exquisite blueberry pie.*

| | | |
|---|---|---|
| All-purpose flour | 1 1/2 cups | 375 mL |
| Icing (confectioner's) sugar | 1/3 cup | 75 mL |
| Butter (or hard margarine), cut up | 3/4 cup | 175 mL |
| Egg yolks (large) | 2 | 2 |
| Ice water | 1 – 2 tbsp. | 15 – 30 mL |
| **BLUEBERRY FILLING** | | |
| Fresh blueberries (or 10 cups, 2.5 L, frozen, thawed and drained well) | 6 cups | 1.5 L |
| Granulated sugar | 2/3 cup | 150 mL |
| Cornstarch | 1/4 cup | 60 mL |
| Finely grated orange zest | 1 1/2 tsp. | 7 mL |
| Orange juice | 2 tbsp. | 30 mL |
| Egg yolk (large), fork-beaten | 1 | 1 |
| Granulated sugar | 2 tsp. | 10 mL |
| **ORANGE SABAYON** | | |
| Large eggs | 2 | 2 |
| Egg yolks (large) | 2 | 2 |
| Granulated sugar | 1 tbsp. | 15 mL |
| Orange juice | 1/4 cup | 60 mL |
| Orange-flavoured liqueur (such as Grand Marnier) | 3 tbsp. | 50 mL |
| Finely grated orange zest | 1 1/2 tsp. | 7 mL |

Process flour, icing sugar and butter in blender or food processor until consistency of coarse crumbs. Transfer to medium bowl.

Stir in egg yolks and just enough ice water to form a ball. Divide into 2 portions. Cover with plastic wrap. Chill for 30 minutes. Roll out large 1/2 of pastry on lightly floured surface to fit ungreased 9 inch (22 cm) pie plate. Carefully lift pastry and press into bottom and up side of pie plate (see page 14). Cover with plastic wrap. Chill for 15 minutes. Roll out second 1/2 of pastry to 1/8 inch (3 mm) thickness. Cover.

**Blueberry Filling:** Combine first 5 ingredients in large bowl. Let stand for 5 minutes. Stir. Turn into shell. Lightly dampen edge of shell with water. Cover with second 1/2 of pastry. Trim and crimp edge to seal.

Brush top and edge of pastry with egg yolk. Sprinkle with second amount of sugar. Cut 5 small slits in pastry to allow steam to escape. Place on baking sheet. Bake on bottom rack in 375°F (190°C) oven for 45 to 50 minutes until golden brown. Serve warm.

**Orange Sabayon:** Whisk first 5 ingredients in heatproof medium bowl over medium saucepan of simmering water until consistency of thin mayonnaise.

Add orange zest. Whisk until well combined. Makes 1 1/2 cups (375 mL) sabayon. Serve immediately with pie. Serves 8.

1 serving: 505 Calories; 23.5 g Total Fat (7 g Mono, 1.4 g Poly, 12.8 g Sat); 238 mg Cholesterol; 66 g Carbohydrate; 4 g Fibre; 7 g Protein; 215 mg Sodium

Pictured on page 145.

## Fig Almond Tart

*This dessert will inspire conversation!*
*Festive-looking tart filled with figs, almonds and*
*some very unique flavourings. Those who enjoy*
*the flavour of licorice will enjoy this treat.*

| | | |
|---|---|---|
| Package of dried figs | 10 oz. | 284 g |
| Water | 5 cups | 1.25 L |
| Package of frozen puff pastry (14 oz., 397 g, size), thawed according to package directions | 1/2 | 1/2 |
| Whipping cream | 1 cup | 250 mL |
| Aniseed, crushed | 3/4 tsp. | 4 mL |
| Fennel seed, crushed | 3/4 tsp. | 4 mL |
| Whole green cardamom, broken | 5 | 5 |
| Egg yolks (large), fork-beaten | 2 | 2 |
| Icing (confectioner's) sugar | 1 tbsp. | 15 mL |
| Ground almonds | 1 tbsp. | 15 mL |
| Whole blanched almonds, toasted (see Tip, page 20) | 1/2 cup | 125 mL |
| Brown sugar, packed | 1 tbsp. | 15 mL |

Combine figs and water in large saucepan. Bring to a boil. Remove from heat. Let stand at room temperature for 2 hours. Drain well. Pat dry. Cut off stems and discard. Slice lengthwise into quarters. Set aside.

Place ungreased 4 x 14 inch (10 x 35 cm) tart pan with removable bottom on ungreased baking sheet. Roll out pastry on lightly floured surface to 6 x 16 inch (15 x 40 cm) rectangle. Carefully lift pastry and press into bottom and up sides of pan (see page 14). Trim edge. Place sheet of parchment paper (or foil) over crust, bringing paper up over sides of pan. Fill halfway up sides with dried beans or rice. Bake in 375°F (190°C) oven for 20 minutes. Crust will not be fully cooked or browned. Carefully remove paper and beans or rice. (These can be kept for next time you are baking pastry.) Cool.

Combine next 4 ingredients in medium saucepan. Bring to a boil on medium-high, stirring often. Reduce heat to low. Simmer for 5 minutes without stirring. Remove from heat. Cool. Strain into small bowl. Discard solids.

Whisk egg yolk, icing sugar and ground almonds into whipping cream mixture. Pour into crust.

Arrange figs, cut side up, over whipping cream mixture. Sprinkle with whole almonds. Sprinkle with brown sugar. Bake in 375°F (190°C) oven for about 30 minutes until whipping cream mixture is puffed and pastry is lightly golden. Let stand on wire rack for 10 minutes. Remove side of pan. Cut tart crosswise into 4 equal pieces. Cut diagonally from 1 corner to opposite corner, making 8 triangles. Serves 8.

1 serving: 412 Calories; 26.7 g Total Fat (9.2 g Mono, 7.3 g Poly, 8.7 g Sat); 90 mg Cholesterol; 41 g Carbohydrate; 4 g Fibre; 7 g Protein; 81 mg Sodium

Pictured on page 147.

Top: Almond Rhubarb Tart, page 148
Bottom: Fig Almond Tart, this page

# Almond Rhubarb Tart

*A moist, cake-like filling tops a rich, buttery crust.*
*Serve cold or at room temperature.*

| Butter (or hard margarine), softened | 1/2 cup | 125 mL |
| Granulated sugar | 1/4 cup | 60 mL |
| Large egg | 1 | 1 |
| All-purpose flour | 1 1/3 cups | 325 mL |
| Salt | 1/4 tsp. | 1 mL |
| **RHUBARB FILLING** | | |
| Strawberry jam, warmed | 1/4 cup | 60 mL |
| Butter (or hard margarine), softened | 1/2 cup | 125 mL |
| Granulated sugar | 1/2 cup | 125 mL |
| Vanilla | 1 tsp. | 5 mL |
| Large eggs | 2 | 2 |
| Ground almonds | 3/4 cup | 175 mL |
| Frozen rhubarb, thawed and drained | 1 cup | 250 mL |
| Sliced almonds | 1/3 cup | 75 mL |
| Apricot jam, warmed and sieved | 2 tbsp. | 30 mL |

Beat butter and sugar in medium bowl until well mixed.

Add egg. Beat well.

Add flour and salt. Mix just until soft dough forms. Cover with plastic wrap. Chill for 30 minutes. Place ungreased 8 inch (20 cm) deep tart pan with removable bottom on ungreased baking sheet. Roll out pastry on lightly floured surface to fit pan. Carefully lift pastry and press into bottom and up side of pan. Trim edge (see page 14). Cover. Chill for 1 hour.

**Rhubarb Filling:** Spread bottom of pastry with strawberry jam.

Beat butter, sugar and vanilla in separate medium bowl until light and creamy.

Add eggs, 1 at a time, beating well after each addition.

Stir in ground almonds and rhubarb. Spread over jam layer.

Sprinkle with sliced almonds. Bake on bottom rack in 350°F (175°C) oven for 40 to 45 minutes until filling is set and crust is golden brown. Let stand in pan on wire rack for 10 minutes.

Carefully brush tart with apricot jam. Cool. Chill for at least 8 hours or overnight. Cuts into 6 to 8 wedges.

*1 wedge: 678 Calories; 43 g Total Fat (15.4 g Mono, 3.3 g Poly, 21.7 g Sat); 195 mg Cholesterol; 67 g Carbohydrate; 2 g Fibre; 10 g Protein; 472 mg Sodium*

Pictured on page 147.

# Rich Chocolate Tart

*A smooth, elegant chocolate tart with a hint of hazelnut in the crust. The perfect finish to a dinner party.*

| **HAZELNUT PASTRY** | | |
| All-purpose flour | 1 cup | 250 mL |
| Icing (confectioner's) sugar | 1/3 cup | 75 mL |
| Finely ground hazelnuts (filberts) | 1/3 cup | 75 mL |
| Butter (or hard margarine), cut up | 1/2 cup | 125 mL |
| Egg yolks (large) | 2 | 2 |
| Ice water | 1 tbsp. | 15 mL |
| **CHOCOLATE FILLING** | | |
| Whipping cream | 1 cup | 250 mL |
| Prepared strong coffee | 1/4 cup | 60 mL |
| Semi-sweet chocolate baking squares (1 oz., 28 g, each), chopped | 16 | 16 |
| Icing (confectioner's) sugar, for dusting | | |
| **CINNAMON CREAM** | | |
| Whipping cream | 2/3 cup | 150 mL |
| Hazelnut-flavoured liqueur (such as Frangelico) | 2 tbsp. | 30 mL |
| Icing (confectioner's) sugar | 2 tbsp. | 30 mL |
| Ground cinnamon | 1/4 tsp. | 1 mL |

**Hazelnut Pastry:** Process first 4 ingredients in blender or food processor until consistency of coarse crumbs. Transfer to medium bowl.

Stir in egg yolks and just enough ice water to form a ball. Place ungreased 10 inch (25 cm) tart pan with removable bottom on ungreased baking sheet. Roll out pastry on lightly floured surface to fit pan. Carefully lift pastry and press into bottom and up side of pan. Trim edge. Cover. Chill for 1 hour. Place sheet of parchment paper (or foil) over crust (see page 14), bringing paper up over side of pan. Fill halfway up side with dried beans or rice. Bake in 375°F (190°C) oven for 15 minutes. Carefully remove paper and beans or rice. (These can be kept for next time you are baking pastry.) Bake for about 10 minutes until lightly browned. Cool.

**Chocolate Filling:** Heat whipping cream and coffee in medium saucepan on medium until bubbles appear around edge. Add chocolate. Heat on lowest heat for about 1 minute, stirring often, until chocolate is almost melted. Do not overheat. Remove from heat. Stir until smooth. Cool for 20 to 30 minutes. Pour into crust. Chill for at least 8 hours or overnight until set. Remove side of pan.

To dust top of tart decoratively, cut thick paper into 12 strips, 1/2 inch (12 mm) wide and 10 inches (25 cm) long. Arrange 6 strips in one direction, 1 inch (2.5 cm) apart, across tart. Repeat with remaining strips in opposite direction to form diamond shapes. Dust liberally with icing sugar. Carefully remove paper strips. Cut tart into 12 wedges.

**Cinnamon Cream:** Beat whipping cream in small bowl until soft peaks form.

Add liqueur, icing sugar and cinnamon. Stir until smooth. Makes 1 1/2 cups (375 mL) cream. Serve with tart. Serves 12.

1 tart serving (without cream): 399 Calories; 29.1 g Total Fat (10 g Mono, 1.2 g Poly, 16.3 g Sat); 82 mg Cholesterol; 37 g Carbohydrate; 3 g Fibre; 4 g Protein; 96 mg Sodium

2 tbsp. (30 mL) Cinnamon Cream: 57 Calories; 4.5 g Total Fat (1.3 g Mono, 0.1 g Poly, 2.8 g Sat); 16 mg Cholesterol; 3 g Carbohydrate; trace Fibre; trace Protein; 5 mg Sodium

Pictured below.

# Fresh Fruit Tart

*This gorgeous dessert will be the hit of any gathering.
Shiny glazed fruit and a refreshing cream top a delicious
cookie dough crust that couldn't be easier to make.
Use holiday cookie dough to match the season.*

### COOKIE CRUST

| | | |
|---|---|---|
| Tube of prepared sugar cookie dough (only about 2/3 of dough will be used) | 18 oz. | 510 g |

### ORANGE CREAM

| | | |
|---|---|---|
| Butter (or hard margarine) | 2 tsp. | 10 mL |
| All-purpose flour | 2 tsp. | 10 mL |
| Orange juice | 1/4 cup | 60 mL |
| Lemon juice | 1 tbsp. | 15 mL |
| Whipping cream | 1/3 cup | 75 mL |
| Egg yolk (large) | 1 | 1 |
| Finely grated orange zest | 3/4 tsp. | 4 mL |
| Finely grated lemon zest | 1/4 tsp. | 1 mL |
| Butter (or hard margarine) | 1/2 cup | 125 mL |
| Icing (confectioner's) sugar | 1/4 cup | 60 mL |
| Assorted fresh fruit (such as blueberries, kiwifruit, peaches and strawberries), cut and sliced as desired, to cover tart (see Note) | | |

### GLAZE

| | | |
|---|---|---|
| Unflavoured gelatin | 1 tsp. | 5 mL |
| White grape juice | 1/2 cup | 125 mL |
| Orange-flavoured liqueur (such as Grand Marnier) or orange juice (optional) | 2 tbsp. | 30 mL |

**Cookie Crust:** Place greased 10 inch (25 cm) tart pan with removable bottom on ungreased baking sheet. Cut cookie dough into 1/8 inch (3 mm) thick slices. Gently press cookie dough slices into bottom and up side of pan. Fill in spaces with quartered slices of cookie dough. Create scalloped edge with halved slices if desired. (Make cookies according to package directions with remaining dough.) Bake in 350°F (175°C) oven for about 15 minutes until golden. Let stand in pan on wire rack to cool.

**Orange Cream:** Melt first amount of butter in small saucepan on medium. Add flour. Mix well. Slowly stir in orange juice, lemon juice and whipping cream. Stir until boiling and thickened. Remove from heat.

Beat egg yolk, orange zest and lemon zest with fork in small cup. Add 1 spoonful hot orange juice mixture. Mix. Add to orange juice mixture. Heat and stir on medium-low for 1 minute. Transfer to small bowl. Cover with plastic wrap directly on surface to prevent skin from forming. Cool to room temperature.

Beat second amount of butter and icing sugar in separate small bowl on high until light and fluffy. Add orange juice mixture. Beat on low until smooth. Makes about 1 1/4 cups (300 mL) cream. Spread evenly in crust.

Arrange fresh fruit over tart. Chill until cold.

**Glaze:** Sprinkle gelatin over grape juice in separate small saucepan. Let stand for 1 minute. Heat and stir on low until dissolved completely.

Stir in liqueur. Cool to room temperature. Carefully spoon about 1/2 of glaze over fruit allowing it to pool in between fruit. (Make sure glaze doesn't flow under cookie crust as it will become soggy.) Chill for about 15 minutes until glaze is set. Spoon remaining glaze over top. Chill until firm. Cuts into 10 wedges.

1 wedge: 410 Calories; 24.5 g Total Fat (10 g Mono, 1.9 g Poly, 11.1 g Sat); 74 mg Cholesterol; 46 g Carbohydrate; 2 g Fibre; 4 g Protein; 330 mg Sodium

Pictured on page 151.

**Note:** Well-drained canned (or frozen, thawed) fruit may also be used.

*Pastries & Tarts*

# Pineapple Meringue Tart

*A fresh, tropical alternative to the traditional lemon meringue. The tart pineapple filling and sweet coconut cookie base give this dessert a summertime feel.*

### COCONUT CRUST

| | | |
|---|---|---|
| Butter (or hard margarine) | 1/3 cup | 75 mL |
| Coconut cookie crumbs (such as Dad's) about 24 cookies | 2 1/2 cups | 625 mL |

### PINEAPPLE FILLING

| | | |
|---|---|---|
| Cornstarch | 3 tbsp. | 50 mL |
| Granulated sugar | 1/3 cup | 75 mL |
| Lemon juice | 2 tbsp. | 30 mL |
| Can of crushed pineapple (with juice) | 14 oz. | 398 mL |
| Butter (or hard margarine) | 3 tbsp. | 50 mL |
| Egg yolks (large), fork-beaten | 3 | 3 |

### MERINGUE TOPPING

| | | |
|---|---|---|
| Egg whites (large), room temperature | 3 | 3 |
| Granulated sugar | 1/2 cup | 125 mL |

**Coconut Crust:** Melt butter in medium saucepan. Remove from heat. Add crumbs. Mix well. Place ungreased 9 inch (22 cm) tart pan with removable bottom on ungreased baking sheet. Press crumb mixture into bottom and up side of pan. Bake in 350°F (175°C) oven for about 10 minutes until golden brown. Let stand in pan on wire rack to cool.

**Pineapple Filling:** Combine cornstarch and sugar in separate medium saucepan. Stir in lemon juice and pineapple with juice. Heat and stir on medium for about 10 minutes until boiling and thickened. Remove from heat.

Add butter. Stir until melted. Add egg yolk. Heat and stir on medium for 1 to 2 minutes until thickened. Pour into crust.

**Meringue Topping:** Beat egg whites in medium bowl until soft peaks form. Gradually add sugar, 1 tbsp. (15 mL) at a time, until sugar is dissolved. Spread over hot filling, sealing to edge of crust. Bake in 350°F (175°C) oven for about 15 minutes until lightly browned. Cool. Chill, uncovered, for 3 hours before serving. Cuts into 8 wedges.

1 wedge: 558 Calories; 23.5 g Total Fat (4.7 g Mono, 0.8 g Poly, 16.4 g Sat); 114 mg Cholesterol; 86 g Carbohydrate; 1 g Fibre; 5 g Protein; 329 mg Sodium

Pictured on page 153.

# Banana Caramel Tart

*A crisp pastry base filled with a sweet caramel custard, bananas and whipped cream. Adults and kids alike will love this dessert. Garnish with banana chips dipped in caramel sugar (see page 181).*

| | | |
|---|---|---|
| Butter (or hard margarine), cut up | 1/2 cup | 125 mL |
| All-purpose flour | 1 1/4 cups | 300 mL |
| Granulated sugar | 2 tbsp. | 30 mL |
| Salt | 1/4 tsp. | 1 mL |
| Egg yolks (large) | 2 | 2 |
| Ice water | 1 – 2 tbsp. | 15 – 30 mL |

### CARAMEL FILLING

| | | |
|---|---|---|
| Brown sugar, packed | 1 cup | 250 mL |
| Butter (or hard margarine), cut up | 2/3 cup | 150 mL |
| Half-and-half cream | 1 cup | 250 mL |
| Spiced rum | 2 tbsp. | 30 mL |
| Water | 2 tbsp. | 30 mL |
| Cornstarch | 3 tbsp. | 50 mL |
| Egg yolks (large) | 2 | 2 |

### BANANA TOPPING

| | | |
|---|---|---|
| Ripe medium bananas, cut into 1/4 inch (6 mm) thick slices | 2 | 2 |
| Whipping cream | 1 cup | 250 mL |
| Long thread (or medium) coconut, toasted (see Tip, page 20) | 2 tbsp. | 30 mL |

Process first 4 ingredients in blender or food processor until consistency of coarse crumbs. Transfer to medium bowl.

Stir in egg yolks and just enough ice water to form a ball. Cover. Chill for 30 minutes. Place greased 9 inch (22 cm) tart pan with removable bottom on ungreased baking sheet. Roll out pastry on lightly floured surface to fit pan. Carefully lift pastry and press into bottom and up side of pan. Trim edge (see page 14). Cover. Chill for 1 hour. Place sheet of parchment paper (or foil) over crust, bringing paper up over side of pan (see page 14). Fill halfway up side with dried beans or rice. Bake in 375°F (190°C) oven for 15 minutes. Carefully remove paper and beans or rice. (These can be kept for next time you are baking pastry.) Bake for about 20 minutes until lightly browned. Cool.

**Caramel Filling:** Heat first 4 ingredients in medium saucepan on medium, stirring constantly, until butter is melted and sugar is dissolved.

Stir water into cornstarch in small cup. Add to brown sugar mixture. Heat and stir on medium-high until boiling and thickened. Remove from heat.

Add egg yolks. Stir until well combined. Cool. Makes about 2 cups (500 mL) filling. Pour into crust. Remove side of pan.

**Banana Topping:** Arrange banana slices in single layer over filling. Beat whipping cream in small bowl until stiff peaks form. Spread evenly over banana slices. Sprinkle with coconut. Cuts into 8 wedges.

1 wedge: 662 Calories; 45 g Total Fat (13.1 g Mono, 1.9 g Poly, 27.2 g Sat); 231 mg Cholesterol; 60 g Carbohydrate; 1 g Fibre; 6 g Protein; 407 mg Sodium

Pictured below.

Top: Pineapple Meringue Tart, page 152
Bottom: Banana Caramel Tart, page 152

# Warm Desserts

Find comfort in these wonderful, freshly baked desserts.
An intimate atmosphere of friends and family is the perfect
backdrop for a warm, inviting custard, a sweet pudding,
a tempting liqueur soufflé, or a fresh-from-the-oven cake.

# Molten Chocolate Cakes

*Chocolate lovers will flip over this temptingly decadent dessert. A rich chocolate filling oozes from the centre of these individually sized cakes.*

| | | |
|---|---|---|
| Butter (or hard margarine) | 2 tsp. | 10 mL |
| Cocoa, sifted if lumpy | 1 tbsp. | 15 mL |
| Butter (not margarine) | 2/3 cup | 150 mL |
| Semi-sweet chocolate baking squares (1 oz., 28 g, each), chopped | 5 | 5 |
| Egg yolks (large) | 2 | 2 |
| Large eggs | 2 | 2 |
| Icing (confectioner's) sugar | 1 1/2 cups | 375 mL |
| All-purpose flour | 1/2 cup | 125 mL |
| Black cherry (or vanilla) ice cream (optional) | | |

Grease six 3/4 cup (175 mL) ramekins with first amount of butter. Coat bottom and side of each ramekin with cocoa, discarding excess cocoa.

Heat second amount of butter and chocolate in small heavy saucepan on lowest heat, stirring often, until almost melted. Do not overheat. Remove from heat. Stir until smooth. Cool slightly.

Beat egg yolks and whole eggs in medium bowl for about 2 minutes until frothy. Beat in icing sugar on low. Add chocolate mixture and flour. Beat well until thick and glossy. Divide batter among prepared ramekins. Place on baking sheet. Bake in 450°F (230°C) oven for about 12 minutes until evenly risen and edge appears set, but middle is still wobbly. Let stand for 3 to 5 minutes. Run knife around side of cakes to loosen. Cover with individual plates and invert to remove from ramekins. (At this point, cakes may sit inverted without removing ramekins for up to 20 minutes. They will stay warm and the centre will still be "molten.") Makes 6 cakes.

To serve, place 2 small scoops of ice cream beside each cake. Serves 6.

1 serving: 525 Calories; 33.6 g Total Fat (10.3 g Mono, 1.6 g Poly, 19.6 g Sat); 206 mg Cholesterol; 55 g Carbohydrate; 2 g Fibre; 6 g Protein; 261 mg Sodium

Pictured below.

# Walnut Chocolate Cakes

*These nutty, brownie-like cakes are drizzled with a rich sauce and a sweet cream. Serve warm for an absolutely delightful dessert.*

| | | |
|---|---|---|
| Walnuts, toasted (see Tip, page 20) | 1 1/2 cups | 375 mL |
| Icing (confectioner's) sugar | 2 cups | 500 mL |
| Cocoa, sifted if lumpy | 1/3 cup | 75 mL |
| All-purpose flour | 1 1/4 cups | 300 mL |
| Egg whites (large), room temperature | 6 | 6 |
| Butter (or hard margarine), melted | 3/4 cup | 175 mL |
| **BUTTERSCOTCH SAUCE** | | |
| Brown sugar, packed | 3/4 cup | 175 mL |
| White corn syrup | 1/2 cup | 125 mL |
| Whipping cream | 1/3 cup | 75 mL |
| Butter (or hard margarine) | 1/4 cup | 60 mL |
| Vanilla | 1 tsp. | 5 mL |
| **BROWN SUGAR CREAM** | | |
| Whipping cream | 1/2 cup | 125 mL |
| Brown sugar, packed | 1 tbsp. | 15 mL |
| Sour cream | 1/3 cup | 75 mL |

Grease muffin pan. Process walnuts in food processor, or place in plastic bag and crush with mallet or rolling pin, until finely chopped. Turn into large bowl.

Add next 3 ingredients. Stir. Make a well in centre.

Beat egg whites in medium bowl until frothy. Add to well. Add butter. Stir well. Divide and spoon into prepared muffin pan. Bake in 375°F (190°C) oven for 20 to 25 minutes until firm and wooden pick inserted in centre of cake is still slightly moist. Let stand in pan for 10 minutes before removing to wire rack. Keep warm. Makes 12 cakes.

**Butterscotch Sauce:** Combine all 5 ingredients in medium saucepan. Heat and stir on medium until sugar is dissolved and butter is melted. Bring to a gentle boil. Boil for 3 to 5 minutes, without stirring, until thickened. Makes 1 1/3 cups (325 mL) sauce.

**Brown Sugar Cream:** Beat whipping cream and brown sugar in small bowl until soft peaks form.

Beat in sour cream until combined. Makes 1 1/4 cups (300 mL) cream. Drizzle warm Butterscotch Sauce over warm cakes. Add dollop of Brown Sugar Cream to each serving. Serves 12.

1 serving: 558 Calories; 32.7 g Total Fat (8.9 g Mono, 7.1 g Poly, 15.1 g Sat); 67 mg Cholesterol; 63 g Carbohydrate; 2 g Fibre; 8 g Protein; 219 mg Sodium

Pictured on page 157.

# Apple Pecan Crisps

*These saucy fruit desserts have a buttery crumb topping and a sprinkling of pecans. The inviting aroma will stimulate your senses.*

| | | |
|---|---|---|
| Butter (or hard margarine), softened | 2 tsp. | 10 mL |
| Large tart cooking apples (such as Granny Smith), peeled and chopped | 2 | 2 |
| Raisins | 1/4 cup | 60 mL |
| Water | 1/2 cup | 125 mL |
| Lemon juice | 2 tsp. | 10 mL |
| Brown sugar, packed | 1/2 cup | 125 mL |
| Cornstarch | 2 tsp. | 10 mL |
| Vanilla | 1/2 tsp. | 2 mL |
| Shortbread cookie crumbs (about 4 cookies) | 1/2 cup | 125 mL |
| Ground cinnamon | 1/8 tsp. | 0.5 mL |
| Butter (or hard margarine) | 2 tbsp. | 30 mL |
| Chopped pecans | 1/4 cup | 60 mL |
| Half-and-half cream (optional) | | |

Grease four 3/4 cup (175 mL) ramekins with first amount of butter.

Combine next 4 ingredients in medium saucepan. Heat on medium, stirring occasionally, until boiling. Simmer, uncovered, on medium-low for about 10 minutes until apple is tender.

Combine brown sugar and cornstarch in small bowl. Stir into apple mixture. Heat and stir on medium for about 3 minutes until boiling and slightly thickened. Remove from heat.

Add vanilla. Stir. Makes about 2 cups (500 mL). Divide apple mixture among prepared ramekins.

Stir crumbs and cinnamon in separate small bowl. Sprinkle over apple mixture.

Melt second amount of butter in small saucepan. Add pecans. Heat and stir on medium until pecans are toasted. Sprinkle over crumb mixture. Bake in 350°F (175°C) oven for about 20 minutes until bubbling.

Drizzle each with cream. Serves 4.

1 serving: 401 Calories; 17.8 g Total Fat (8.1 g Mono, 2.3 g Poly, 6.5 g Sat); 25 mg Cholesterol; 62 g Carbohydrate; 2 g Fibre; 2 g Protein; 178 mg Sodium

Pictured below.

Top Left: Apple Pecan Crisps, page 156

Bottom Centre: Walnut Chocolate Cakes, page 156

# Maple Apple Fritters

*These golden, battered rings of apple are sprinkled with cinnamon and served with a sweet Maple Cream. The flavours are warm and oh, so comforting!*

### MAPLE CREAM

| | | |
|---|---|---|
| Maple (or maple-flavoured) syrup | 1/2 cup | 125 mL |
| Sour cream | 1/2 cup | 125 mL |
| Brown sugar, packed | 1/3 cup | 75 mL |
| Whipping cream | 1 cup | 250 mL |
| All-purpose flour | 1 1/2 cups | 375 mL |
| Granulated sugar | 2 tbsp. | 30 mL |
| Salt | 1/4 tsp. | 1 mL |
| Large eggs | 2 | 2 |
| Beer | 1 cup | 250 mL |
| Cooking oil | 2 tbsp. | 30 mL |
| Granulated sugar | 1/3 cup | 75 mL |
| Ground cinnamon | 1/2 tsp. | 2 mL |
| Large tart cooking apples (such as Granny Smith) | 3 | 3 |
| Cooking oil, for deep-frying | | |

**Maple Cream:** Combine first 3 ingredients in medium saucepan. Heat and stir on medium until sugar is dissolved. Bring to a gentle boil. Boil for 2 to 3 minutes, without stirring, until slightly thickened. Cool completely.

Beat whipping cream in small bowl until soft peaks form. Add maple mixture. Stir. Cover. Chill. Makes 2 1/2 cups (625 mL) cream.

Combine flour, first amount of granulated sugar and salt in large bowl. Make a well in centre.

Add next 3 ingredients to well. Mix well. Cover. Let stand at room temperature for 2 hours.

Combine second amount of granulated sugar and cinnamon in separate small bowl.

Core and peel apples, leaving apples whole. Cut into 1/3 inch (1 cm) thick slices (you will need 32 slices). Dip individual slices into batter. Deep-fry, in batches, in hot (375°F, 190°C) cooking oil for about 2 minutes until golden brown and crisp. Remove to paper towels to drain. Sprinkle with cinnamon mixture. Serve with Maple Cream. Serves 8.

1 serving: 518 Calories; 26.6 g Total Fat (11.5 g Mono, 4.5 g Poly, 9 g Sat); 96 mg Cholesterol; 64 g Carbohydrate; 2 g Fibre; 5 g Protein; 116 mg Sodium

Pictured on page 159.

# Lemon Sponge Custard

*This light dessert has a golden, cake top with a creamy lemon custard bottom. Try this warm or cold—it's delicious either way!*

| | | |
|---|---|---|
| Butter (or hard margarine), softened | 3 tbsp. | 50 mL |
| Granulated sugar | 3/4 cup | 175 mL |
| Salt | 1/4 tsp. | 1 mL |
| Egg yolks (large) | 4 | 4 |
| All-purpose flour | 1/4 cup | 60 mL |
| Milk | 1 cup | 250 mL |
| Lemon juice | 1/3 cup | 75 mL |
| Finely grated lemon zest | 1 tbsp. | 15 mL |
| Egg whites (large), room temperature | 4 | 4 |
| Boiling water | | |

Grease six 3/4 or 1 cup (175 or 250 mL) ramekins. Beat first 3 ingredients in large bowl until well combined.

Add egg yolks, 1 at a time, beating well after each addition.

Add flour. Stir.

Add next 3 ingredients. Whisk gently to remove any lumps.

Beat egg white in medium bowl until stiff (not dry) peaks form. Fold egg whites into lemon mixture. Do not overmix. Gently spoon into prepared ramekins. Place in baking pan. Carefully pour enough boiling water into baking pan to come halfway up side of ramekins. Bake in 325°F (160°C) oven for 35 to 40 minutes until tops are puffed and golden. Let stand in pan on wire rack for 15 minutes before serving. Serves 6.

1 serving: 246 Calories; 9.7 g Total Fat (3.1 g Mono, 0.7 g Poly, 5 g Sat); 161 mg Cholesterol; 35 g Carbohydrate; trace Fibre; 6 g Protein; 222 mg Sodium

Pictured on page 159.

Top: Lemon Sponge Custard, above
Bottom: Maple Apple Fritters, this page

# Sticky Ginger Fig Cake

*The warm, comforting undertones in this
golden brown, flat-topped cake are complemented
by the lightly spiced caramel sauce. Delicious!*

| Water | 1 1/3 cups | 325 mL |
| Chopped dried figs | 1 1/3 cups | 325 mL |
| Baking soda | 1 tsp. | 5 mL |
| Butter (or hard margarine), softened | 1/3 cup | 75 mL |
| Brown sugar, packed | 2/3 cup | 150 mL |
| Large eggs | 2 | 2 |
| All-purpose flour | 1 cup | 250 mL |
| Baking powder | 2 tsp. | 10 mL |
| Minced crystallized ginger | 1/4 cup | 60 mL |

### CINNAMON BRANDY SAUCE

| Butter (or hard margarine), cut up | 1/2 cup | 125 mL |
| Brown sugar, packed | 1/2 cup | 125 mL |
| Whipping cream | 1/2 cup | 125 mL |
| Brandy | 2 tbsp. | 30 mL |
| Ground cinnamon | 1/2 tsp. | 2 mL |

Grease deep round 8 inch (20 cm) cake (or springform) pan. Line bottom and side with parchment (not waxed) paper (see page 12). Bring water to a boil in medium saucepan. Add figs. Remove from heat. Add baking soda. Stir. Let stand for 10 minutes. Process in blender or food processor until almost smooth.

Beat butter and brown sugar in large bowl until creamy and sugar is dissolved. Add eggs, 1 at a time, beating well after each addition.

Combine next 3 ingredients in medium bowl. Add to butter mixture. Stir well. Add fig mixture. Stir well. Pour batter into prepared pan. Bake in 350°F (175°C) oven for about 50 minutes until wooden pick inserted in centre comes out clean. Let stand in pan for 10 minutes before turning out onto wire rack to cool. Cut into 8 wedges.

**Cinnamon Brandy Sauce:** Combine all 5 ingredients in medium saucepan. Heat and stir on medium until butter is melted and sugar is dissolved. Bring to a gentle boil. Boil for about 5 minutes, without stirring, until slightly thickened. Cool slightly. Makes 1 cup (250 mL) sauce. Drizzle over individual servings of warm cake. Serves 8.

1 serving: 540 Calories; 27.1 g Total Fat (7.9 g Mono, 1.3 g Poly, 16.3 g Sat); 127 mg Cholesterol; 72 g Carbohydrate; 4 g Fibre; 5 g Protein; 500 mg Sodium

Pictured on page 161.

# Peach Bourbon Dessert

*This grilled cake looks so inviting when served with
the delicious peach sauce and a scoop of vanilla ice cream.
This recipe is so easy to make. It's the perfect thing to
whip together when unexpected guests drop by.*

| Butter (or hard margarine) | 2 tbsp. | 30 mL |
| Brown sugar, packed | 2 tbsp. | 30 mL |
| Bourbon whiskey | 1 tbsp. | 15 mL |
| Frozen pound cake, thawed | 10 1/2 oz. | 298 g |
| Cans of sliced peaches (in juice), 14 oz. (398 mL) each | 2 | 2 |
| Butter (or hard margarine) | 1/4 cup | 60 mL |
| Brown sugar, packed | 1/4 cup | 60 mL |
| Bourbon whiskey | 2 tbsp. | 30 mL |
| Cornstarch | 1 tbsp. | 15 mL |

Heat first 3 ingredients in small saucepan on medium, stirring constantly, until butter is melted.

Preheat electric grill for 5 minutes or gas barbecue to medium. Peel or cut top crust off cake. Cut crosswise into 6 slices. Cut each slice in half diagonally. Brush both sides of each slice liberally with bourbon mixture. Place on well-greased grill. Cook for 2 to 3 minutes per side until golden brown.

Drain juice from peaches into medium saucepan. Set peaches aside. Add remaining 4 ingredients to juice. Heat on medium for about 5 minutes, stirring constantly, until boiling and thickened. Add peaches. Stir until heated through. Makes about 4 cups (1 L). Serve with cake. Serves 6.

1 serving: 384 Calories; 12.7 g Total Fat (3.6 g Mono, 0.7 g Poly, 7.6 g Sat); 33 mg Cholesterol; 62 g Carbohydrate; 2 g Fibre; 4 g Protein; 304 mg Sodium

Pictured on page 161.

Top: Peach Bourbon Dessert, above
Bottom: Sticky Ginger Fig Cake, this page

# Pear Date Cake

*This warm cake contains bits of pear and dates.*
*The sweet hint of butterscotch and the distinct maple*
*flavour in the sauce make a comforting combination.*

| | | |
|---|---|---|
| Water | 1 cup | 250 mL |
| Chopped dates | 1 cup | 250 mL |
| Baking soda | 1 tsp. | 5 mL |
| Butter (or hard margarine), softened | 1/3 cup | 75 mL |
| Brown sugar, packed | 2/3 cup | 150 mL |
| Large eggs | 2 | 2 |
| All-purpose flour | 1 cup | 250 mL |
| Baking powder | 2 tsp. | 10 mL |
| Chopped (fresh or canned) peeled pear | 1 1/2 cups | 375 mL |

**MAPLE SAUCE**

| | | |
|---|---|---|
| Maple (or maple-flavoured) syrup | 1/2 cup | 125 mL |
| Butter (or hard margarine), cut up | 1/2 cup | 125 mL |
| Whipping cream | 1/2 cup | 125 mL |

Grease deep 8 × 8 inch (20 × 20 cm) cake (or springform) pan. Bring water to a boil in medium saucepan. Add dates. Remove from heat. Add baking soda. Stir. Let stand for 10 minutes. Process in blender or food processor until almost smooth.

Beat butter and brown sugar in large bowl until creamy and sugar is dissolved. Add eggs, 1 at a time, beating well after each addition.

Combine next 3 ingredients in medium bowl. Add to butter mixture. Stir well. Add date mixture. Stir well. Pour batter into prepared pan. Bake in 350°F (175°C) oven for about 50 minutes until wooden pick inserted in centre comes out clean. Let stand in pan for 10 minutes before turning out onto wire rack to cool. Cut into 8 pieces.

**Maple Sauce:** Combine all 3 ingredients in medium saucepan. Heat and stir on medium until butter is melted. Bring to a gentle boil. Boil for about 5 minutes, without stirring, until slightly thickened. Makes about 1 1/3 cups (325 mL) sauce. Drizzle over individual servings of warm cake. Serves 8.

1 serving: 512 Calories; 26.9 g Total Fat (7.8 g Mono, 1.2 g Poly, 16.2 g Sat); 127 mg Cholesterol; 67 g Carbohydrate; 3 g Fibre; 4 g Protein; 492 mg Sodium

Pictured this page.

Left: Pear Date Cake, above
Right: Bananas In Pastry, page 164

# Bananas In Pastry

*Crisp, pastry-like crusts encase firm bananas.*
*For a unique presentation, cut each half into diagonal*
*slices, drizzle with sauce and dust with icing sugar.*
*Leftover sauce can be stored in the refrigerator.*

## CREAMY CARAMEL SAUCE

| | | |
|---|---|---|
| Granulated sugar | 1 cup | 250 mL |
| Water | 1/3 cup | 75 mL |
| Whipping cream | 1 cup | 250 mL |
| Large flour tortillas (10 inch, 25 cm, diameter) | 4 | 4 |
| Butter (or hard margarine), melted | 3 tbsp. | 50 mL |
| Brown sugar, packed | 2 tbsp. | 30 mL |
| Granulated sugar | 1 tbsp. | 15 mL |
| Ground cinnamon | 1 tsp. | 5 mL |
| Firm medium bananas | 4 | 4 |
| Cooking oil, for deep-frying | | |

**Creamy Caramel Sauce:** Combine first amount of granulated sugar and water in medium saucepan. Heat and stir on medium for about 5 minutes until starting to boil and sugar is dissolved. Brush down sugar crystals several times with brush dipped in water. Boil for 5 to 10 minutes, without stirring, until deep golden brown. Watch carefully and immediately remove from heat once colour is reached (see page 16).

Carefully drizzle whipping cream slowly into caramel in steady stream, whisking constantly, until combined. Bring to a boil on medium. Cook and stir for about 1 minute until sauce is smooth. Makes 1 1/3 cups (325 mL) sauce.

Brush 1 side of each tortilla generously with butter.

Combine next 3 ingredients in small cup. Sprinkle evenly over butter.

Trim 1 banana to fit on centre of 1 tortilla, leaving 1 1/2 inch (3.8 cm) edge on each side of banana. Roll up tightly, folding in ends. Secure by pushing wooden picks through tortilla into ends of banana. Use 1 or 2 wooden picks to secure long side of tortilla. Repeat with remaining tortillas and bananas.

Deep-fry packages, in 2 batches, in hot (375°F, 190°C) cooking oil for about 2 minutes until golden on all sides. Remove to paper towels for about 2 minutes until cooled slightly. Remove and discard wooden picks. Cut in half on sharp diagonal. Arrange 2 pieces on each of 4 individual plates drizzled with about 2 tbsp. (30 mL) sauce. Drizzle with remaining sauce. Serves 4.

1 serving: 882 Calories; 47 g Total Fat (18.3 g Mono, 6.5 g Poly, 19.8 g Sat); 97 mg Cholesterol; 115 g Carbohydrate; 3 g Fibre; 6 g Protein; 317 mg Sodium

Pictured on page 163.

# Flaming Sauced Bananas

*Firm pieces of banana rest in a buttery liqueur sauce*
*speckled with cinnamon. Serve as a filling for Basic Dessert*
*Crêpes, page 93, or over vanilla ice cream. Yum!*

| | | |
|---|---|---|
| Butter (or hard margarine) | 1/4 cup | 60 mL |
| Brown sugar, packed | 1/2 cup | 125 mL |
| Ground cinnamon | 1/2 tsp. | 2 mL |
| Whipping cream | 1/4 cup | 60 mL |
| Firm medium bananas, cut into 1 inch (2.5 cm) pieces | 3 | 3 |
| Banana-flavoured liqueur (such as Crème de Banane) | 1/4 cup | 60 mL |
| Amber (or dark) rum | 1/3 cup | 75 mL |

Melt butter in large frying pan on medium. Stir in brown sugar and cinnamon. Heat and stir until bubbling and sugar is melted.

Stir in whipping cream.

Add banana. Stir until banana is coated. Remove from heat.

Heat liqueur and rum in small saucepan on medium until quite warm. Carefully pour onto banana mixture in frying pan. Heat on medium, shaking pan back and forth 2 or 3 times. Ignite surface with match. Shake pan back and forth several times until flame extinguishes. Spoon sauce over banana until coated. Makes 2 1/2 cups (625 mL). Serves 6.

1 serving: 305 Calories; 11.9 g Total Fat (3.4 g Mono, 0.5 g Poly, 7.3 g Sat); 34 mg Cholesterol; 38 g Carbohydrate; 1 g Fibre; 1 g Protein; 96 mg Sodium

Pictured on page 165.

# Chocolate Liqueur Soufflés

*A hint of hazelnut liqueur flavours these
chocolate brown soufflés. For the best results,
serve this light, fluffy dessert immediately.*

| | | |
|---|---|---|
| Butter (or hard margarine), softened | 1/2 tsp. | 2 mL |
| Granulated sugar | 1 – 2 tbsp. | 15 – 30 mL |
| Butter (or hard margarine) | 2 tbsp. | 30 mL |
| All-purpose flour | 2 tbsp. | 30 mL |
| Hazelnut-flavoured liqueur (such as Frangelico) | 1/4 cup | 60 mL |
| Milk | 3 tbsp. | 50 mL |
| Semi-sweet chocolate baking squares (1 oz., 28 g, each), chopped | 3 | 3 |
| Egg yolks (large) | 3 | 3 |
| Granulated sugar | 3 tbsp. | 50 mL |
| Egg whites (large), room temperature | 3 | 3 |

Cocoa, for dusting

Grease four 1/2 cup (125 mL) ramekins with first amount of butter. Coat bottom and side of each ramekin with first amount of sugar, discarding excess sugar. Place ramekins on baking sheet.

Melt second amount of butter in small saucepan on medium. Add flour. Heat and stir for about 1 minute until bubbling.

Add liqueur and milk. Stir until combined.

Add chocolate. Heat and stir until chocolate is almost melted. Remove from heat. Stir until smooth.

Add egg yolks and second amount of sugar. Stir. Turn into large bowl.

Beat egg white in medium bowl until soft peaks form. Fold 1/3 of egg white into chocolate mixture until almost combined. Add remaining egg white. Fold in until just combined. Do not overmix. Carefully spoon mixture into prepared ramekins.

Run thumb around inside edge of ramekins in soufflé mixture to ensure even rising during baking. Bake in 375°F (190°C) oven for 12 to 15 minutes until puffed.

Dust with cocoa. Serve immediately. Serves 4.

1 serving: 337 Calories; 16.6 g Total Fat (5.4 g Mono, 1 g Poly, 8.9 g Sat); 179 mg Cholesterol; 36 g Carbohydrate; 1 g Fibre; 6 g Protein; 121 mg Sodium

Pictured on page 167.

When making soufflés, folding in egg whites is a very important step. Use metal spoon with a thin edge to fold in the egg whites. It won't deflate the air bubbles in mixture in the same way a thick wooden spoon will. Use a light touch and don't overmix. Folding in egg whites properly is a crucial point in making well-risen soufflés.

# Doughnut Pudding

*This adults-only dessert is the perfect finish to
a dinner party. The spices in the pudding
are complemented by the flavourful Bourbon Sauce.*

| | | |
|---|---|---|
| Diced dried apricots | 1/3 cup | 75 mL |
| Golden raisins | 1/4 cup | 60 mL |
| Warm brandy (or orange juice) | 1/4 cup | 60 mL |
| Large eggs | 5 | 5 |
| Can of evaporated milk (not skim) | 13 1/2 oz. | 385 mL |
| Half-and-half cream (or homogenized milk) | 1/2 cup | 125 mL |
| Brown sugar, packed | 1/3 cup | 75 mL |
| Vanilla | 1 tsp. | 5 mL |
| Ground cinnamon | 1 tsp. | 5 mL |
| Ground nutmeg | 1 tsp. | 5 mL |
| Cubed day-old (or stale) glazed doughnuts (about 4 large) | 4 cups | 1 L |
| **BOURBON SAUCE** | | |
| Butter (not margarine) | 3/4 cup | 175 mL |
| Brown sugar, packed | 1 1/2 cups | 375 mL |
| Bourbon whiskey | 1/3 cup | 75 mL |
| Whipping cream | 1 cup | 250 mL |

Combine apricots, raisins and brandy in small bowl. Let stand for 30 minutes.

Beat next 7 ingredients in large bowl.

Add doughnuts. Stir until coated. Let stand for 5 minutes. Fold in apricot mixture. Turn into greased 2 quart (2 L) casserole. Bake in 350°F (175°C) oven for about 50 minutes until puffed and set. Let stand for 15 minutes to cool slightly.

**Bourbon Sauce:** Melt butter in medium saucepan on medium. Add brown sugar and bourbon. Heat and stir for about 2 minutes until sugar is dissolved.

Add whipping cream. Stir until warm. Makes 2 2/3 cups (650 mL) sauce. Spoon about 1/4 cup (60 mL) sauce over each serving of warm pudding. Serve remaining sauce in pitcher on the side. Serves 6.

1 serving: 1095 Calories; 61.6 g Total Fat (21.6 g Mono, 3.6 g Poly, 32.6 g Sat); 324 mg Cholesterol; 112 g Carbohydrate; 2 g Fibre; 15 g Protein; 605 mg Sodium

Pictured on page 169.

**CINNAMON BUN PUDDING:** Omit doughnuts. Use same amount of stale cinnamon buns.

# Croissant Strawberry Pudding

*This rich, creamy pudding has tender pieces
of croissant baked into it. The combination tastes
like warm French toast and strawberry jam.*

| | | |
|---|---|---|
| Strawberry jam | 1/3 cup | 75 mL |
| Medium croissants, halved horizontally | 4 | 4 |
| Egg yolks (large) | 6 | 6 |
| Large eggs | 3 | 3 |
| Half-and-half cream | 3 cups | 750 mL |
| Granulated sugar | 1/2 cup | 125 mL |
| Strawberry ice cream topping | 1/3 cup | 75 mL |

Icing (confectioner's) sugar, for dusting

Grease 2 1/2 quart (2.5 L) casserole. Spread jam onto cut side of each croissant. Cut each half into 3 pieces. Place, jam side up, in prepared casserole.

Beat next 5 ingredients in large bowl until well combined. Carefully pour over croissants. Place in large roasting pan. Let stand for 15 minutes. Carefully pour enough boiling water into roasting pan to come halfway up side of casserole. Bake in 325°F (160°C) oven for about 1 hour until set. Remove from roasting pan. Let stand for about 15 minutes to cool slightly.

Just before serving, dust with icing sugar. Serve warm. Serves 8.

1 serving: 424 Calories; 21.3 g Total Fat (6.6 g Mono, 1.5 g Poly, 11.1 g Sat); 294 mg Cholesterol; 50 g Carbohydrate; 1 g Fibre; 10 g Protein; 289 mg Sodium

Pictured on page 169.

Top and Bottom: Doughnut Pudding, this page
Centre Right: Croissant Strawberry Pudding, above

# Finishing Touches

This instructive section is full of ideas on how to bring clever artistry to your dessert creations. Look for helpful information on decorating techniques, elegant garnishes and dazzling plate presentations. Your guests will be impressed by the spectacular results.

# Finishing Tools

1. Ribbon
2. Parchment paper
3. Decorative foil paper – for covering cake boards
4. Ruler
5. Scissors
6. Fine strainer – for dusting cocoa or icing sugar
7. Small offset spatula
8. Paring knife
9. Lazy susan
10. Ice cream scoops - various sizes
11. Graters
12. Small brushes – for making sugared flowers
13. Marble slab – for cooling chocolate filigrees or chocolate collars
14. Cream horn molds – for shaping tuile cornets
15. Coupler
16. Various piping tips
17. Small piping bag
18. Pencil
19. Pastry brush
20. Triangle cake comb
21. Paper doilies
22. Zester/Channeler – for making citrus zest and curls
23. Vegetable peeler – for making chocolate curls and shavings
24. Hammer
25. Parchment paper cone
26. Large squeeze bottle – for sauces
27. Small squeeze bottle – for sauces
28. Long cake comb – for decorating top of cakes
29. Metal skewer
30. Wooden picks

# Icing Cakes

*Transform a plain cake from ordinary to extraordinary with these easy-to-follow icing techniques. Once you are familiar with these simple skills, have fun experimenting and creating your own unique styles.*

To prevent cake crumbs from mixing with icing, spread very thin layer of buttercream over top and sides of cake. Let stand until set. Smooth with more buttercream.

Cover top and sides of cake with desired amount of buttercream. Use offset spatula or spatula held at slight angle against cake to smooth over side.

**Swirling:** Using offset spatula or spatula, create peaks and swirls over top and around side of cake.

**Combing:** Using cake comb, serrated knife or fork, make wavy lines on top of cake.

**Note:** Use a Lazy Susan to make cake easier to decorate.

# Edging Cakes

*These dazzling edging techniques will give your cakes a beautiful finished look. Use them sparingly for a touch of understated elegance, or use them in combination with a decorative icing technique for over-the-top decadence.*

**Textured Edge:** Ice cake with about 1/4 inch (6 mm) thickness of icing or glaze. Using plain or serrated cake comb or scraper, slowly turn cake in a continuous steady motion in 1 direction while you hold the comb steady against side of cake. Carefully lift off comb to create a clean seam.

**Crumbed Edge:** Place un-iced cake on small cake board (page 184). Ice with about 1/4 inch (6 mm) thickness of icing or glaze. While icing is still sticky, balance cake on 1 hand and gently press coarsely grated chocolate, chopped nuts or praline (see page 132) into icing around edge.

# Simple Collars

*Collars are a creative way to edge a cake. This technique requires a bit more time, but the end result is both unique and stunning.*

Cut 4 pieces of parchment (not waxed) paper, 3 1/4 x 12 inches (8 x 30 cm) each. Spread melted chocolate evenly onto paper. Let stand until set. Cut crosswise into 1 1/2 inch (3.8 cm) pieces. Makes 32 tiles.

Press chocolate tiles, slightly overlapping, around outside edge of cake.

# Advanced Collars

*This decorative collar is easier to make than you might think. Chocolate collars are fun to look at and even more fun to eat. This extra touch is perfect for a special occasion.*

Cut piece of parchment (not waxed) paper same height as cake and long enough to go around circumference of cake plus 1/2 inch (12 mm) for "tab." Secure paper to counter with tape.

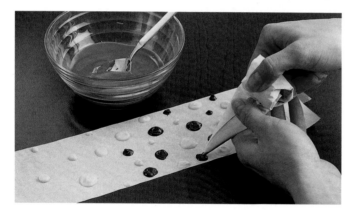

Pipe melted white and semi-sweet chocolate dots, in various sizes, randomly onto parchment paper. Let stand for about 2 minutes until both chocolates are set.

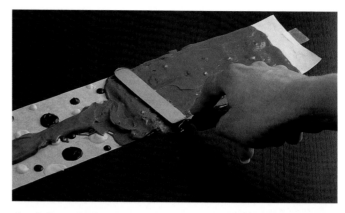

Carefully spread melted milk chocolate onto parchment paper over chocolate dots with offset spatula, leaving "tab" uncovered. Let stand for 1 to 4 minutes to set slightly, but still be pliable. If chocolate becomes too set for shaping, use low setting on hair dryer to warm chocolate until pliable enough.

Working quickly, wrap collar around cake, gently pressing ends to meet together. Do not remove paper. Let stand for 1 hour until chocolate is firm.

Carefully peel off and discard paper.

# Pretty Piping

*Turn a plain-looking dessert into a showpiece with these easy piping techniques. The right tools and a steady hand are all you need to create these beautiful designs.*

**Assembling Coupler:** Push coupler base into piping bag until bottom 2 threads are exposed. Coupler base should fit snugly in bag. Select decorating tip and position over bag and coupler. Place coupler ring over tip and tighten to secure.

## Piping Tips:

1. Medium Plain Tip: Dots, pearls, beads and kisses
2. Open Star Tip: Stars, shells and rosettes
3. Rose Tip: Ruffles, roses and rosebuds
4. Basket Weave Tip: Ribbed or plain stripes and basket weave designs
5. Small Open Star Tip: Stars, shells and rosettes
6. Small Plain Tip: Writing, dots, pearls, beads and lines

**Stars:** Fill piping bag fitted with small closed star tip. Squeeze bag gently as you lift up and away to make small stars.

**Rosettes:** Fill piping bag fitted with small open star tip. Squeeze bag gently as you pipe in a small circular motion on cake to create rosette.

**Borders:** Fill piping bag fitted with small closed star tip. Position tip at bottom edge of cake. Squeeze bag as you lift slightly and drag bag/icing backward to create shell pattern. Each shell should measure about 1 inch (2.5 cm) in length.

# Making A Paper Cone

*If you don't have a piping bag of your own, don't worry! In five simple steps, you can make a sturdy, disposable piping bag out of a single sheet of paper. What could be easier?*

Cut out 10 inch (25 cm) square from parchment (or waxed) paper. Fold in half diagonally to form triangle. Hold longest side of triangle in middle with your left hand. Fold bottom corner up and over to meet middle corner (opposite your left hand). Roll about 2 inches (5 cm) of paper under to form cone shape. Hold in position.

Fold top corner down, around and behind first fold. Adjust top corner until it meets point of middle corner. Pull back corner down slightly to form very tight point.

Fold pointed edge over several times to secure seam (or secure with stapler).

Fill piping bag 1/3 full with icing or melted chocolate. Pinch open end together between thumbs and forefingers to close. Fold top edge over once. Fold each top corner in to meet in middle. Fold top edge over again.

Snip very small piece from point of cone to make small hole. Start with a very small hole—you can always make it bigger if necessary.

# Chocolate Garnishes

*Melt it, mold it, shape it, sculpt it—chocolate is a fun, versatile decorating ingredient with an unmistakable, dramatic elegance.*

**Chocolate Leaves:** Use pliable leaves with well-defined veins, such as mint, lemon or salal, available at most florist shops. Be sure leaves are clean and dry. Hold leaf, underside up, in 1 hand. Using small brush, coat layer of melted chocolate on leaf. Place, coated-side up, on waxed paper on plate. Chill until set.

Carefully peel leaf away from chocolate.

**Grated Chocolate:** Working against grater, hold both grater and chilled chocolate firmly, letting chocolate shreds fall onto piece of waxed paper. Use different sides on grater to achieve different looks.

**Chocolate Curls:** Peel room temperature chocolate firmly along its length with sharp vegetable peeler. For narrower curls, use flat underside of peeler.

**Filigree Shapes:** Half fill small piping bag fitted with smallest plain tip with melted chocolate. Pipe patterns or shapes onto parchment (or waxed) paper-lined baking sheet. Or with a pencil, trace a shape onto parchment (or waxed) paper. Turn paper over and pipe chocolate over designs. Let stand until set. Carefully lift chocolate designs off paper with thin metal spatula.

**Chocolate Filigree:** Tape parchment (or waxed) paper onto rolling pin. Drizzle melted chocolate back and forth over curve of rolling pin. Let stand until set. Carefully peel paper from chocolate design.

# Tuile Tricks

*French for "tiles," tuiles (TWEELS) are thin, delicate cookies that are rolled or shaped and sometimes dipped in chocolate. Enjoy them on their own or use them to add a touch of flair to your desserts.*

**To Make:** Line baking sheet with parchment (not waxed) paper. Trace circles, slightly apart, on paper. Turn paper over. Measure batter into each circle. Using offset spatula, spread batter thinly and evenly to fill circles. Bake until lightly browned.

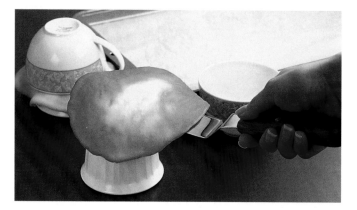

**Tuile Baskets:** Working quickly, slide spatula under each warm cookie. Place over upside-down ramekin (or cup). Carefully press another ramekin over circle to form basket shape. Let stand for about 5 minutes until cool and crisp. Remove ramekins.

**Rolled (Cigarette) Tuiles:** Working quickly, slide spatula under each warm cookie. Place under pencil (or wooden spoon handle). Roll around pencil to form tight cylinder. Let stand for 2 to 3 minutes until cool and crisp before sliding off.

**Curved Tuiles:** Working quickly, slide spatula under each warm cookie. Place on rolling pin to cool completely. Dip edge of each tuile in melted chocolate if desired.

**Cornets:** Working quickly, slide spatula under each warm cookie. Place, pan-side down, on parchment paper cone (or cream horn mold). Roll around cone, using tea towel to protect your hands. Let stand for about 2 minutes until cool and crisp before removing from cone.

Using offset spatula, spread batter thinly and evenly to fill in shape. Remove template. Bake until lightly browned.

Working quickly, slide spatula under each cookie. Remove to wire rack to cool.

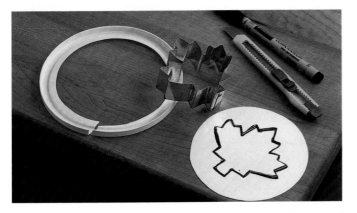

**Tuile Cut-Out:** Trace desired shape on thin, round piece of cardboard (or plastic lid). Carefully cut out shape and discard. Place template on parchment (not waxed) paper-lined baking sheet. Measure batter into centre of template.

&

- Having 2 baking sheets and 2 sheets of parchment paper with drawn circles helps this process go much faster. As soon as you remove tuiles from oven, place the other pan in to bake while you form the rolls. Then get another set ready on the cooled parchment paper.

- Tuiles may be warmed in oven on baking sheet if they become too hard to shape.

# Sugar Shapes

*These eye-catching toffee shapes will add a decorative touch to any recipe. Their beautiful amber colour is a striking complement to any dessert.*

**Drizzling:** Drizzle hot sugar syrup (see page 16) onto greased baking sheet into small shapes and squiggles. Let stand for about 20 minutes until hard. Carefully remove from tray using pancake lifter or offset spatula.

**Shards (Broken Glass):** Pour sugar syrup onto greased foil-lined baking sheet. Carefully tilt pan to spread mixture thinly and evenly. Let stand for about 20 minutes until hard.

Break into pieces.

# Coconut Curls

*Infuse your desserts with a taste of the tropics by garnishing them with a few strategically placed coconut curls.*

**Piercing Eyes:** Pierce holes through eyes of coconut, using metal skewer.

**Removing Flesh:** Crack coconut with hammer into 3 inch (7.5 cm) pieces. Pry coconut flesh from shell, using dull knife.

**Making Curls:** Peel coconut into strips, using vegetable peeler.

# Fancy Fruit

*Your guests will "ooh" and "aah" at
these dazzling fruit garnishes.*

**Candied Citrus Zest:** Heat and stir equal parts sugar and water in small frying pan on low until sugar is dissolved. Bring to a boil. Add slices of citrus fruit (see Note). Boil for 3 to 5 minutes, without stirring, until slightly thickened, but not coloured. Drain slices and lightly coat with berry sugar or remove directly to wire rack to cool.

**Toffee Fruit:** Dip pieces of fruit (see Note) into sugar syrup (see page 16). Transfer to parchment (not waxed) paper-lined baking sheet. Let stand until set. Do not refrigerate.

**Chocolate Dipped Fruit:** Dip pieces of fruit (see Note) into melted white, milk or dark chocolate. Transfer to parchment (not waxed) paper-lined baking sheet. Let stand until set.

# Frosted Fruit & Flowers

*We mean it when we say that these fruit
and flowers are pretty enough to eat!*

**Frosted Flowers:** Brush edible flowers (or petals) with egg white or meringue powder mixed with water. Hold wet flowers over bowl of berry sugar. Lightly sprinkle with sugar. Let stand on wire rack to set.

Some suggestions for edible flowers: borages, calendulas, carnations, chamomiles, chrysanthemums, citrus blossoms, dandelions, gardenias, Johnny jump-ups, lavenders, pansies, nasturtiums, marigolds, roses and violets.

**Sugared Fruit:** Brush small pieces of fruit, such as grapes and gooseberries, with egg white or meringue powder mixed with water. Place wet fruit in bowl of berry sugar. Lightly sprinkle with sugar. Let stand on wire rack until set.

**Note:** Use very thin slices of citrus fruits, such as limes, oranges, lemons or kumquats. Use firm fruit for dipping, such as berries, grapes, banana chips, dried apricots or star fruit slices.

# Plate Presentation

*These ornamental techniques are a great way to dress up individual serving plates. Try to enhance what you are serving by choosing a presentation that best complements the dessert.*

## Quick and Easy Sauces:

1. Red Currant Jelly
2. Raspberry Jelly
3. Apricot Preserves
4. Strawberry Jelly
5. Caramel Sauce

6. Grape Jelly
7. Strained Cherry Pie Filling
8. Apple Jelly
9. Chocolate Sauce
10. Mint Jelly

**Two-Sauce Bull's Eye:** Squeeze dark-coloured sauce or chocolate around edge of plate to make 1 to 1 1/2 inch (2.5 to 3.8 cm) border. Squeeze light-coloured sauce into centre until just touching dark sauce. Starting from outer edge of light sauce, drag wooden pick in straight line through sauce towards centre. Continue at 1/4 inch (6 mm) intervals.

**Dragging Hearts:** Squeeze dark-coloured sauce or chocolate onto centre of plate. Combine 3 tbsp. (50 mL) sour cream and 1 to 2 tbsp. (15 to 30 mL) water in small bowl. Carefully drop about ten 1/8 tsp. (0.5 mL) dots of sour cream mixture at even intervals, about 1/2 inch (12 mm) in from edge of sauce (an eye dropper works very well for this). Position point of wooden pick in sauce between 2 dots. Drag wooden pick through centre of first dot and continue around plate, not lifting or stopping until you have gone all the way around plate.

**Two-Sauce Swirl:** Carefully spoon 2 complementing sauces, such as caramel and chocolate, raspberry and chocolate, or coffee and vanilla, onto separate halves of plate. Carefully swirl wooden pick through darker sauce and then through lighter sauce at 1 inch (2.5 cm) intervals.

**Drizzle Design:** Fill 2 separate piping bags (or paper cones, page 176) with 2 different colours of melted chocolate. Pipe first colour in drizzle pattern onto plate. Move plate 1/8 turn. Drizzle with second colour. Let stand until set before topping with dessert.

**Piped Design Filled With Sauce:** Spoon melted white, milk or dark chocolate into piping bag fitted with a small plain tip. Pipe design, onto outer edge of plate. Let stand until set. Add sauce of your choice, such as caramel or raspberry sauce, to fill in shape or parts of shape.

**Star Design:** Pipe star design around outer edge of plate. Add dot between each point. Let stand until set before topping with dessert.

**Sauce Border:** Squeeze small dots of assorted sauce colours around edge of plate. Position point of wooden pick in centre of 1 dot. Drag wooden pick through centre of first dot and continue around plate, not lifting or stopping until you have gone all the way around plate.

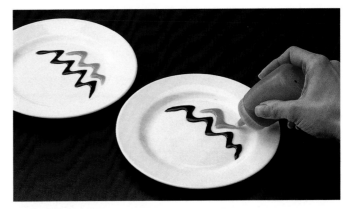

**Sauce Squiggles:** Squeeze squiggle pattern down 1 side of plate with first sauce. Squeeze smaller squiggle beside first with second sauce.

**Dusting Over Object:** Hold object, such as fork, about 1/2 inch (12 mm) over plate. Sprinkle cocoa over plate and object (or sprinkle with icing sugar if plate is a dark colour). Carefully remove object.

# Creating Cake Boards

*The great thing about cake boards is that you can customize their size and shape to perfectly fit your cake. Select paper and ribbon that suit the style of your cake, as cake boards can be a beautiful decorative addition to the overall appearance of your dessert.*

**Equipment:** Foam board 1/3 to 1/2 inch (1 to 1.2 cm) thick, ruler, pencil, utility knife, scissors, pins, paper or cloth for covering board and ribbon for edge of board.

**Measuring Board:** Measure out size of cake board required on foam board. Place foam board on cutting board. Cut out foam board with utility knife.

**Covering Board:** Place paper (or cloth), wrong-side up, on work surface. Place foam board on top of paper. Cut around board, leaving 2 inch (5 cm) border of excess paper. Fold paper over board.

Secure paper to board with tape.

**Edging Board:** Measure ribbon to fit around edge of cake board. Secure ribbon around edge with pins.

# Measurement Tables

*Throughout this book measurements are given in Conventional and Metric measure. To compensate for differences between the two measurements due to rounding, a full metric measure is not always used. The cup used is the standard 8 fluid ounce. Temperature is given in degrees Fahrenheit and Celsius. Baking pan measurements are in inches and centimetres as well as quarts and litres. An exact metric conversion is given on this page as well as the working equivalent (Standard Measure).*

## Oven Temperatures

| Fahrenheit (°F) | Celsius (°C) | Fahrenheit (°F) | Celsius (°C) |
|---|---|---|---|
| 175° | 80° | 350° | 175° |
| 200° | 95° | 375° | 190° |
| 225° | 110° | 400° | 205° |
| 250° | 120° | 425° | 220° |
| 275° | 140° | 450° | 230° |
| 300° | 150° | 475° | 240° |
| 325° | 160° | 500° | 260° |

## Spoons

| Conventional Measure | Metric Exact Conversion Millilitre (mL) | Metric Standard Measure Millilitre (mL) |
|---|---|---|
| 1/8 teaspoon (tsp.) | 0.6 mL | 0.5 mL |
| 1/4 teaspoon (tsp.) | 1.2 mL | 1 mL |
| 1/2 teaspoon (tsp.) | 2.4 mL | 2 mL |
| 1 teaspoon (tsp.) | 4.7 mL | 5 mL |
| 2 teaspoons (tsp.) | 9.4 mL | 10 mL |
| 1 tablespoon (tbsp.) | 14.2 mL | 15 mL |

## Cups

| | | |
|---|---|---|
| 1/4 cup (4 tbsp.) | 56.8 mL | 60 mL |
| 1/3 cup (5⅓ tbsp.) | 75.6 mL | 75 mL |
| 1/2 cup (8 tbsp.) | 113.7 mL | 125 mL |
| 2/3 cup (10⅔ tbsp.) | 151.2 mL | 150 mL |
| 3/4 cup (12 tbsp.) | 170.5 mL | 175 mL |
| 1 cup (16 tbsp.) | 227.3 mL | 250 mL |
| 4 1/2 cups | 1022.9 mL | 1000 mL (1 L) |

## Pans

| Conventional Inches | Metric Centimetres |
|---|---|
| 8 x 8 inch | 20 x 20 cm |
| 9 x 9 inch | 22 x 22 cm |
| 9 x 13 inch | 22 x 33 cm |
| 10 x 15 inch | 25 x 38 cm |
| 11 x 17 inch | 28 x 43 cm |
| 8 x 2 inch round | 20 x 5 cm |
| 9 x 2 inch round | 22 x 5 cm |
| 10 x 4 1/2 inch tube | 25 x 11 cm |
| 8 x 4 x 3 inch loaf | 20 x 10 x 7.5 cm |
| 9 x 5 x 3 inch loaf | 22 x 12.5 x 7.5 cm |

## Dry Measurements

| Conventional Measure Ounces (oz.) | Metric Exact Conversion Grams (g) | Metric Standard Measure Grams (g) |
|---|---|---|
| 1 oz. | 28.3 g | 28 g |
| 2 oz. | 56.7 g | 57 g |
| 3 oz. | 85.0 g | 85 g |
| 4 oz. | 113.4 g | 125 g |
| 5 oz. | 141.7 g | 140 g |
| 6 oz. | 170.1 g | 170 g |
| 7 oz. | 198.4 g | 200 g |
| 8 oz. | 226.8 g | 250 g |
| 16 oz. | 453.6 g | 500 g |
| 32 oz. | 907.2 g | 1000 g (1 kg) |

## Casseroles

### Canada & Britain

| Standard Size Casserole | Exact Metric Measure |
|---|---|
| 1 qt. (5 cups) | 1.13 L |
| 1 1/2 qts. (7 1/2 cups) | 1.69 L |
| 2 qts. (10 cups) | 2.25 L |
| 2 1/2 qts. (12 1/2 cups) | 2.81 L |
| 3 qts. (15 cups) | 3.38 L |
| 4 qts. (20 cups) | 4.5 L |
| 5 qts. (25 cups) | 5.63 L |

### United States

| Standard Size Casserole | Exact Metric Measure |
|---|---|
| 1 qt. (4 cups) | 900 mL |
| 1 1/2 qts. (6 cups) | 1.35 L |
| 2 qts. (8 cups) | 1.8 L |
| 2 1/2 qts. (10 cups) | 2.25 L |
| 3 qts. (12 cups) | 2.7 L |
| 4 qts. (16 cups) | 3.6 L |
| 5 qts. (20 cups) | 4.5 L |

# How-To Index

# Recipe Index

"The last bite tasted is
the first one remembered."

Jean Paré